# DESIGNING & REMODELING
# BATHROOMS

Created and designed by
the editorial staff of
*ORTHO BOOKS*

**Project Editor**
Jill Fox

**Writer**
Robert Be[...]

**Photogra[...]**
Kenneth

**Illustrat[...]**
Rik Olson

D1275887

# Ortho Books

*Publisher*
Edward A. Evans

*Editorial Director*
Christine Jordan

*Production Director*
Ernie S. Tasaki

*Managing Editors*
Michael D. Smith
Sally W. Smith

*System Manager*
Linda M. Bouchard

*National Sales Manager*
J. D. Gillis

*National Accounts Manager—
  Book Trade*
Paul D. Wiedemann

*Marketing Specialist*
Dennis M. Castle

*Distribution Specialist*
Barbara F. Steadham

*Operations Assistant*
Georgiann Wright

*Administrative Assistant*
Francine Lorentz-Olson

*Senior Technical Analyst*
J. A. Crozier, Jr., Ph.D.

Address all inquiries to:
Ortho Books
Box 5006
San Ramon, CA 94583-0906

Copyright © 1982, 1990
Monsanto Company
All rights reserved under international and Pan-American copyright conventions.

9  10  11  12  13
95  95  97  98  99  00

ISBN 0-89721-215-0
Library of Congress Catalog Card
Number 89-85930

**THE SOLARIS GROUP**
2527 Camino Ramon
San Ramon, CA 94583-0906

# Acknowledgments

*Bathroom Consultants*
Fred Brasch, Superior Remodeling,
  Oakland, Calif.
Claire Carter, design consultant,
  Oakland, Calif.
Dan Fuller, Dan Fuller Construction,
  Berkeley, Calif.
Lyndell Hogan, House of Kitchens,
  Albany, Calif.
Bob Lombardi, Lombardi Construction,
  Sebastopol, Calif.
David Newton, National Kitchen
  & Bath Association
Don Riley, Heritage Woodworks,
  St. Helena, Calif.
Lee Seronnello, Kitchen & Bath Designs,
  Napa, Calif.
Lois Shamberger and Kathleen Donohue,
  Neil Kelly Construction,
  Portland, Oreg.
Beverly Wilson, design consultant,
  Berkeley, Calif.

*Special Thanks to*
Linda Beckstrom

*Photography Assistants*
Norma Bontadelli
Melissa McCumiskey

*Copy Chief*
Melinda E. Levine

*Editorial Coordinator*
Cass Dempsey

*Copyeditor*
Irene Elmer

*Proofreader*
Stephen McElroy

*Indexer*
Elinor Lindheimer

*Editorial Assistants*
Deborah Bruner
Theresa Lewis
Tamara Mallory
John Parr

*Composition by*
Nancy McCune
Laurie A. Steele

*Production by*
Lezlly Freier

*Separations by*
Color Tech Corp.

*Lithographed in the USA by*
Banta Company

*Front cover:* Adding a fancy leaded window gave this guest bathroom a stunning focal point. Lighting is a dynamic design element. Look for ways to bring in as much natural light as possible, then supplement it with artificial light to complete your lighting plan.

*Page 1:* A brightly colored sink adds a delightful dimension to even the simplest bathroom. Color is an important design element. It can transform a space and give it much of its character.

*Page 3:* Remodeling a bathroom is a process of combining functional needs and decorative elements into a cohesive design. Don't forget the items that put your personal touch on the room—a stained glass window, a portable TV, or both.

*Back cover*
*Top left:* Whirlpool tubs and separate oversized shower stalls are popular features in master bathrooms. These luxury items add to the comfort of the owners and the resale value of the house.

*Top right:* Special painting techniques, such as the sponging style in this bathroom, give dimension to walls. Sponging involves painting the room twice: once with a light-colored base coat using standard tools, and then a second time with a darker shade using a sponge.

*Bottom left:* Wallcovering is a traditional decorating method for bathrooms. Many manufacturers provide fabric for curtains, ceramic tile, and other accessories to match wallcoverings. This pedestal sink has been painted to match the surrounding walls, creating a beautifully coordinated bathroom.

*Bottom right:* A stripe of bright hand-painted tiles enliven this otherwise all monochromatic room. The tile work was designed by the homeowner and executed by a ceramic artist. Specialty tiles are a great way to personalize a room.

# DESIGNING & REMODELING
# BATHROOMS

# PREFACE

Today's homeowners want a refuge, a quiet place where they can escape the hectic pace of the working world and the demands of family life for a few precious moments of comfort. To achieve this, more and more people are remodeling their bathrooms.

Bathrooms have changed; once merely a convenient room for personal hygiene, the bath has become a private retreat meant for pampering and relaxation. Privacy has always been a requirement for bathrooms, but now it is dictated by life-style as much as by modesty. Once standardized and banal, bathrooms are now showplaces of unique design and personal expression.

In days of old, high styling and chic decorating were confined to the formal, public spaces of a home—the living room, dining room, parlor, and entry. Eventually the bedrooms, family room, and kitchen began to receive the same lavish attention. Now the bathroom has come of age as an arena for dramatic design that goes far beyond utilitarian necessity. Entering a modern bathroom, you no longer feel as though you had left home and landed on another planet. The distinctions between bathroom and other rooms are disappearing; so much so that the master bathroom is often used as a private living room and the family bathroom may now sport the same color scheme, flooring, wallcoverings, and furniture as adjacent rooms. Even tiny powder rooms and guest bathrooms receive the same attention as luxurious bathing suites.

Why such changes? One reason is social: People see the home as a special place for focusing and centering their lives. Another reason is economic: Whereas families used to move up the home-buying ladder, they are now more likely to stay put and make major improvements on their present home, usually starting with the kitchen and bathroom.

Bathrooms also represent the flip side of a trend toward more open spaces where families can enjoy time together. When kitchens are used as gathering places and formal living rooms are giving way to multipurpose family rooms, adults want a private comfort zone of their own to shut out the pressures and stress of the busy workplace and the busy home. The bathroom, a uniquely personal and private room, fulfills this need.

As people are more body conscious, with increasing honesty and frankness, we pay more attention to personal hygiene and physical conditioning than ever before. People are also discovering the therapeutic value of daily bathing, as much for mental as for physical relaxation—a secret that the Japanese and Finns have known for centuries.

In recent years bathrooms have become more eclectic and less likely to follow any single trend. In some instances walls have opened up and the bathroom has become part of a bedroom or sitting room or even part of the outdoors. In other instances various functions have become more separate and compartmentalized. But in all instances there is a desire to transform a strictly functional, sterile box into a room as exciting and personal as any other area in the home.

As you think about your own bathroom project—whether it is sprucing up the existing bathroom or designing a part of a new home—you will want it to be as pleasant, efficient, and beautiful as possible. Creating such a bathroom is what this book is all about.

The success of any building project depends on careful designing, thorough planning, and accurate work. Even if you hire out the entire project and do none of the work yourself, you will find that it goes much more smoothly if you are prepared to participate as much as possible.

This book will guide you through a complete bathroom project. The first chapter offers an overview of the design process. It presents ideas and techniques for planning the overall design, using your present bathroom as a starting point.

The second chapter presents more specific design ideas. It helps you to refine the plan and to choose various fixtures, finish materials, and details.

The third chapter is a practical guide for planning the construction phase of the project. It will help you to establish a realistic time line; to estimate the cost; to work with professionals; and to deal with codes, permits, and inspections.

The fourth chapter is a comprehensive construction guide. It contains step-by-step instructions for dismantling the old bathroom; roughing in the structural, plumbing, and electrical work; preparing the finish surfaces; and installing new fixtures and accessories. It focuses on tasks that are unique to bathrooms, but it includes summary information about more general skills, such as carpentry, plumbing, and wiring.

This book should help you to enjoy the process of creating a new and exciting bathroom. Read through the entire book before starting your project. The planning will be easier if you understand the details of construction and installation, and knowing the basics about design will make the construction easier, too.

*Opposite: The average adult spends an hour a day in the bathroom. To make the most of this time, a bathroom should be well lit, well heated, and well ventilated, and it should be decorated in colors you enjoy.*

# BATHROOM DESIGN

Successful bathroom designs make creative use of the available space, combine the various elements into an integrated and satisfying whole, and reflect your own personal style. To achieve these results, you must make a patient and careful search for solutions to particular problems. Whether designing a new room or remodeling an existing bathroom, the design process usually involves the same steps. You must survey the existing space, establish a design style, lay out the fixture locations, and choose finishing materials. This chapter takes you through these steps and presents criteria for planning the basic layout.

Planning is the most important step in the entire remodeling process, so be sure to give yourself plenty of time. It will take weeks, even months, to design a new bathroom and prepare for construction. If you plan to use professional help, you should still complete as many of the preliminary steps as possible. The project will go more smoothly if you do.

*Small bathrooms lend themselves to the use of fine materials. A few feet of marble tile give this family bathroom a feeling of luxury. A stylish bathroom will add to the overall enjoyment—and resale value—of your home.*

# GETTING STARTED

**B**egin by gathering information; assessing the present bathroom; setting goals and priorities for the new room; and evaluating the realities of the remodeling project in terms of cost, codes, and the structural integrity of your home. To clarify your ideas, you must make many decisions, and you must always be ready to refine and revise your plans.

## Gathering Ideas

One of your first, and most enjoyable tasks will be to gather ideas. Start with the ideas in this book. Then set up a filing system to help you to organize your various notes, clippings, and brochures. An accordion file works very well because it will also hold bulky items, such as magazines and samples of materials. File folders, scrapbooks, and 3-ring binders are also useful for organizing information. Use categories suggested by the page headings and checklists in this book, or devise your own system of classification.

If you gather more ideas than you can use, don't be afraid to winnow them out. Just be sure to save product specifications and installation instructions that you will need later on.

There are many sources of information. You may already subscribe to one or two magazines devoted to the home, or you can pick up a cartfull of them at your supermarket or newsstand. The feature articles and the advertisements offer hundreds of innovative ideas and plans. Some magazines are devoted exclusively to kitchens and bathrooms.

Trade publications are distributed only to the professionals; you may find them in a large public library or in an architect's or contractor's office. Often they showcase products that are not advertised to the general public. Manufacturers are another good source of information. They offer color brochures, specification sheets, installation instruction sheets, and lists of local dealers. Look for an address or a contact in their magazine advertisements. Or check your local library for a copy of *Sweet's Catalog*. This multivolume compilation of manufacturer's brochures is designed for quick reference.

Retail stores and showrooms are a fine source of information about specific products. Bathroom specialists often have showrooms, as do plumbing suppliers, home improvement centers, and other dealers. They may sell only to contractors and other professionals, or they may have a limited selection of brands, but they can still give you many good ideas. Ask if they have a portfolio of local bathroom projects that you can browse through.

Model homes, open houses, and home tours are another good source of hands-on information. Bring a tape measure and a pencil and paper so you can take notes. If you like to travel, you may also find exciting ideas in small inns, hotels, or bed-and-breakfast establishments.

Do not overlook the homes of your friends and family, especially if they have new or remodeled bathrooms. Unlike showrooms, these are real installations, so you can look under the sink, behind the walls, and in the attic and the basement to see how units are installed. Ask these homeowners whether they like or dislike various features and why. You can also ask them to recommend qualified professionals if you do not intend to do all the work yourself.

## Assessing the Space

While you're gathering information from other sources, examine the present bathroom. Even though it has features that you don't like, it may have other features that you want to retain or to modify only slightly. The Bathroom Survey (see page 12) will help you to assess your bathroom needs in terms of light, space, storage, layout, and other amenities. You will need this information in order to create your new design.

You will also need a floor plan of the existing space (see page 19) to use as a starting point for new layouts. Draw up this floor plan before you do the survey. It provides an additional tool for making notes and gives you a chance to verify critical dimensions. If you work with design professionals, doing these tasks prior to meeting with them will streamline the process and make you more knowledgeable about your own project.

## Setting Priorities

The notes you took when you were gathering ideas and your answers on the Bathroom Survey will help you to set your design goals for the new bathroom. Some items are obvious—things that have annoyed you for a long time probably motivated you to remodel in the first place—but you may have discovered other items that are equally important. Do not eliminate anything yet, even things that you don't think can be changed.

Now rank all these items in order of their importance to you. This list will help you to make design decisions and establish budget priorities. It will help you to keep things in perspective if you become frustrated by

*Opposite: Before you begin your bathroom design, make a list of all the things you want from the new room. A roomy, well-lit shower obviously topped this homeowner's list.*

a stubborn problem or dazzled by a decorator showcase. It will also help you to see where you can make trade-offs when you are faced with limited space or a tight budget or both. For instance, would you rather have two basins and a shower or one basin and a tub? Two basins side by side or a separate shower and tub? A brand-new tub or the old one and a skylight? Keep the list handy so that you can revise it and refer back to it from time to time. It will change as you gain more information and absorb new ideas.

## Considering the Realities

Up to this point the design possibilities are wide open. You have been gathering information and setting goals, perhaps dealing only with distant dreams and vague possibilities. Now it is time to identify the practical issues that will set limits on the design. These are the hard realities: budget, building codes, the physical and structural limitations of the space, the feasibility of changing plumbing and wiring, and the amount of work you intend to do yourself. Do not view these issues as obstacles to creating a wonderful design—view them rather as opportunities for creative problem solving.

### Budget

Generally speaking, a new bathroom costs about as much as a new car. It is a major capital expenditure, and the amount you spend depends on whether you want an economy pickup truck or a luxury touring sedan. If you select inexpensive materials and do all the work yourself, you can probably remodel your present bathroom for less than $5,000. On the other hand, you could spend the same amount on a luxury bathtub alone. Before you begin, you should have some idea of what you're willing to spend. Investigate all your financing options. Will you take out an

equity home loan? Home-improvement loan? A loan against certain assets? Establish as firm and realistic a figure as possible. Cost overruns are common in remodeling, so allow for them by establishing a budget that is lower than your reserves. When you come up with a few preliminary designs, you can hire a general contractor to make an estimate or you can make your own (see pages 62–63). The results may send you back to the drawing board, but it is only by moving back and forth between plans and estimates that you will be able to set a firm budget and stay within its limits. Remember that a beautiful and well-designed bathroom will enhance the value of your home, so the money you spend on a new bathroom is an investment.

### Doing It Yourself

The design may be affected by the amount of planning and construction work you want to do yourself. Assess your own skills and interest as soon as possible. After reading this book you will have a good idea of what is involved in each step of the remodeling process.

You may want to work out the design, do the preliminary planning, and manage the construction without actually doing any of the work. Or you may want to do all of the demolition and only some of the other jobs yourself and hire out for the more complicated construction work. By knowing what you want to do and being realistic about your skills, you can adjust the design to take advantage of your strengths and avoid costly procedures that are beyond your abilities.

### Codes and Permits

In most municipalities and counties, a remodeling project is subject to certain codes. Depending on the type and scope of the work, these may include the zoning, building, plumbing, electrical, mechanical, and possibly energy codes. Visit your local planning or building inspection department and discuss your project

with the appropriate officials to find out what codes pertain and what permits will be required. Ask whether you will need prior approval from another agency, such as the sanitation department.

Zoning and design restrictions apply to changes in the exterior of the house. Unless your project involves an addition or exterior alterations, it will probably not be subject to these restrictions.

It will be subject to the building code if there are structural changes, or if the project exceeds a certain amount of money. In either case you will probably have to get a permit. The building code covers structural and safety issues related to the actual construction. For a bathroom remodeling, this is likely to include any framing or structural alterations, minimum ceiling heights, clearance below beams, size of doorways, type of window glass, height of steps, and clearances around fixtures.

Plumbing, electrical, and mechanical codes cover all the work done in these respective areas, although replacing existing fixtures without moving the plumbing or wiring usually does not require a permit. However, you may be required to bring the existing plumbing and wiring up to code even if you are not altering any of it. This is always a good idea anyway; it increases the safety and enhances the value of your home.

It is not necessary to understand every detail of the codes. Just be aware that they will govern some aspects of the design and construction. The fourth chapter covers many of the specific code requirements pertaining to bathrooms, but you should also consult with your local building inspection department. If you hire professionals to do the work, they will be responsible for obtaining permits, following the codes, and getting all the necessary inspections.

## Structural Issues

If you wish to move a wall, add a window, install a skylight, remove the ceiling, or add onto the existing house, you will need to know whether the proposed work is structurally feasible. Some alterations, such as adding a doorway or a window, involve only simple changes in the framing. Other alterations entail major structural changes. Examples include installing large French doors in an exterior wall, removing ceiling joists, and moving a bearing wall. If you are installing a new luxury tub or adding extensive marble or tile, you may have to reinforce the floor. A large soaking tub full of water, with two people in it, can weigh as much as 1200 pounds.

To determine whether a change is feasible, ask yourself the following questions: Does it involve walls that support overhead loads? Will a double top plate have to be broken? Must rafters or ceiling joists be altered? Are the floor joists sized properly and do they run in the right direction? Does the foundation provide adequate support? Is there enough lateral support for large openings? Is there any rot or similar damage to account for? You will probably not be able to analyze all of these factors yourself, so get professional advice before making a final decision. On the other hand, do not rule out changes just because they seem complicated. You may be surprised to find out what is possible.

### Plumbing and Wiring

In any bathroom remodeling project there is always the potential for extensive and costly changes in the plumbing and wiring. These could involve upgrading the entire plumbing system or adding new circuits to the breaker panel. But changes in the plumbing and wiring are not always costly. Plastic pipes and fittings have streamlined the modern plumber's work considerably.

Quite often the biggest cost factor is access rather than materials. If you have a clear crawl space or basement below the bathroom and easy access to the attic above, you may be able to make extensive changes at relatively little cost. If you are planning to gut the bathroom, to add insulation or to resurface all the walls, you may also be able to alter the plumbing and wiring very easily. Restricting the plumbing fixtures to one wall or to two adjacent walls may make changes simpler, too. It is impossible to know exactly what is involved until you talk with the person who will be doing the actual work, but you can begin by seeing whether the drainpipes, water supply pipes, and wiring runs are reasonably accessible. After you have read the guidelines in the fourth chapter, you will have a better idea of what to look for.

*A one-piece toilet and a pedestal sink take up less space than more conventional fixtures and so are good choices for smaller rooms.*

# The Bathroom Survey

Whether you're planning simply to rejuvenate one or two features of your existing bathroom, to rip it apart completely and start over from scratch, or to add a bathroom as part of a new home or addition, the following questions will help you to identify the problems that you want to correct and the overall style elements that you want to incorporate. Bear in mind that there is no wrong answer to any of these questions. If the survey asks you to think about a problem and you find yourself thinking about a solution instead, go ahead and note down the solution. Obviously, the questions are not exhaustive. The purpose of the survey is to help you to focus on particular problem areas of the existing bathroom and to stimulate creative solutions for the new room.

The short lists that follow the questions are intended as a review of common bathroom elements, divided into the survey categories.

## General Considerations

Who uses the bathroom? When? Do certain members of the household use it at the same time? Is it used by anyone who has special needs, such as a youngster or a disabled person? Will there be changes in the family in the near future (new baby coming, a grown-up child leaving home)? Do visitors use this bathroom? Overnight guests? Is the bathroom used for other activities (developing photos, washing the family dog, gardening, laundry)? Can these activities be done elsewhere? Have you any long-range plans for remodeling your home? Do they include the addition of another bathroom?

☐ Number of users
☐ Ages of users
☐ Special needs of users
☐ Additional room uses
☐ Future room needs
☐ Privacy considerations

## Overall Design

As you enter the bathroom, what are your first impressions? Do you like the way it looks? What do you like and dislike about it? Is it too bright? Too dark? Too small? Too sterile? Too boring? Cold? Garish? Cramped? Old-fashioned? Somber? Spacious? As you list the characteristics you like and dislike, note the particular elements—color, light, or style—that contribute to the atmosphere that you want.

☐ Overall impression
☐ Current style
☐ Style of adjoining rooms
☐ Features to retain
☐ Problem features to eliminate

## Space, Traffic, and Layout

Is there enough space in the bathroom for the people and activities that must be accommodated? If not, why not? For instance, are too many people using a limited number of fixtures? Are secondary activities, such as exercise, laundry, or pet care, taking up valuable space? Is there enough counter space? Enough mirror area? Enough privacy? Does the door swing into the room and take up useful space? Are there any wasted areas? Which fixture is used most frequently? (It's usually the washbasin.) Is it easy to get to? Is there more than one entrance to the bathroom? Is it necessary to have more than one? Is there space next to the bathroom for expansion—an extra closet, a dead-end hallway, or an extra large bedroom, for example? Are dressing areas close to the bathroom? Are laundry facilities convenient?

☐ Current fixtures
☐ Desired fixtures
☐ Can space be expanded
☐ Door swing direction
☐ Minimum clearances achieved

## Storage

Is there enough storage space? Is it efficient? Are there items that you don't need to store in the bathroom? Are there items that you'd like to store in the bathroom but don't have room for? Is the room messy because there is no organized storage space for towels, toothbrushes, and so forth? Do you prefer open storage or closed storage? Do you like to display towels or keep them hidden?

☐ Towel storage
☐ Linen storage
☐ Bulk paper product storage
☐ Appliance storage
☐ Safe medicine storage
☐ Safe cleaning product storage
☐ Storage accessibility

## Heating

Is the bathroom warm enough? Too warm? What is the heat source? Can it be moved or changed if necessary? If you are not satisfied with the heating system, what changes would you like to make?

☐ Type of heat
☐ Type of ventilation
☐ Noise considerations

## Finish Surfaces

What are the wall-, ceiling-, and floor coverings? What do you like and dislike about these materials? Are they easy or hard to keep clean? Have they chipped, peeled, mildewed, cracked, or deteriorated in any other way? Are the colors satisfactory? Have the surfaces worn well? Would you want to use these same materials again?

☐ Wall finishes
☐ Floor finishes
☐ Ceiling finishes
☐ Shower surround
☐ Bathtub surround
☐ Are finishes sound
☐ Are colors compatible

## Fixtures and Fittings

In bathrooms, the word *fixtures* generally refers to the washbasin, toilet, tub, shower, and bidet. The word *fittings* generally refers to the faucets, handles, exposed pipes, and similar hardware. What do you like and dislike about each fixture and fitting? Do they look dated? Are they easy to use? Are the colors satisfactory? Are they difficult to clean? Would you prefer a single-control faucet where you now have two-handled faucets? Would you prefer two faucets where you now have one? Do you wish to keep any fixtures or fittings? If you wish to replace any, do you have a particular replacement in mind?

☐ Washbasin style
☐ Faucet style
☐ Shower style
☐ Shower head style
☐ Bathtub style
☐ Toilet style
☐ Are fixtures sound
☐ Are fittings sound

## Accessories and Hardware

The small details often make or break a bathroom design. Consider what items you have in your present bathroom and what items you may want to add. Are there any items that you don't have and want? Are there any items that you have and don't use? Are your present accessories conveniently located? Do you like the colors, materials, and design?

☐ Mirror
☐ Laundry hamper
☐ Towel bars
☐ Clothes hooks
☐ Toothbrush holder
☐ Toilet paper holder
☐ Door handles
☐ Drawer pulls
☐ Book or magazine rack
☐ Wastebasket
☐ Soap dishes
☐ Rug

## Lighting and Electrical Outlets

Are there any sources of natural light? If so, during what part of the day is the room brightest? In what direction does the window face? Is there wall space where a window would be appropriate (this is often the case in tract homes)? Is there enough privacy? Is there enough artificial light? Is it incandescent or fluorescent? Is the light too harsh? Too soft? Does it shine where you need it the most? Do you like the fixtures? Are there enough electrical outlets? Where are they located? Do you need additional outlets for hair dryers, curling irons, and electric razors convenient to the place where they are used and to a mirror? Are the outlets designated GFCI (ground fault circuit interrupter) as is required in bathrooms? What electrical fixtures (fan, heater, ventilator, heat lamp) are permanently installed? Are you satisfied with their locations? If not, what changes would you suggest?

☐ Number of windows
☐ Window sizes
☐ Available views
☐ Skylight possibilities
☐ Decorative light fixtures
☐ Additional light sources
☐ Number of electrical outlets
☐ Outlet positions
☐ Currently installed appliances
☐ Desired installed appliances
☐ Small appliances used regularly
☐ Laundry facilities

## Special Needs

Are there people in your household who have or who soon may have special needs? Children? Elderly adults? Someone who is disabled? Someone who is exceptionally tall or short? Is the toilet at a comfortable height? Are there grab bars near the toilet, tub, and shower? Can children be bathed without discomfort to the person who is doing the bathing? Is the door wide enough to take a wheelchair? Can children reach the faucets? Is the sink low enough or high enough for everyone in the household? Is there space underneath it for wheelchair use? Is there provision for sitting in the shower?

☐ Installed grab bars
☐ Sink height and position
☐ Toilet style and type
☐ Special bathing needs
☐ Bathtub height
☐ Shower head height
☐ Door width for special access
☐ Check minimum clearances

## Luxuries

Are there any luxury fixtures in or adjacent to the bathroom, such as a whirlpool bath, steam cabinet, hot tub, or sauna? Will the existing plumbing and electrical capacity handle these luxuries? Is there a television, radio, stereo (or speakers), telephone, or intercom in the room? Should you consider installing any of these things when you plan the rewiring? How about space for plants, an aquarium, or a birdcage? Would you like to have any of these? Where would you put them?

☐ Whirlpool bath
☐ Sauna
☐ Intercom
☐ Telephone
☐ Television with remote control
☐ Radio or stereo with speakers
☐ Will circuit handle new needs
☐ Pet needs

# DESIGNING WITH STYLE

There are no absolutes in good bathroom design. There are only pragmatic issues and aesthetic issues. It all boils down to one question: Is the design optimally functional and do you like the way it looks?

Function is the basic building block of the design. It defines how well the bathroom meets practical needs and determines such factors as layout, storage, and location of fixtures.

Some of the design is generated by the space itself. A good design highlights the best features of the room and plays down the worst features. If the room is large and light and has an enormous panoramic view, a good design will focus on the window. On the other hand, if the window opens on a dusty air shaft, it makes sense to obscure the view (but not the light or ventilation).

Beyond these practical considerations, however, is the aesthetic impact of the room, which can range from animated, dramatic, and spectacular to understated, peaceful, and serene. Your choices here are a matter of personal taste and style. Design is a very individual thing.

There is no right or wrong style. However, it is important to know what your style is and how various elements contribute to it or detract from it. Even when you are sketching basic floor plans—putting the tub here or the washbasin there—your design will go much more smoothly if you have a clear idea of the look and tone you are trying to achieve.

You may not realize it, but you already have a style. Whether you own a large house or a small condominium, you have made some decisions about the way your space is presented: You like dark colors or light ones, modern furnishings or antiques, simple or complex shapes. Maybe you like your style and don't want to change it; maybe you want to develop an entirely new style. You can do either of these things as you design your new bathroom.

First look through the photographs in this book and in your file. They should serve as a starting point in defining your style. Some may appeal to you immediately; others may leave you cold. Look at the details as well as the overall picture. You may find a complete bathroom that you like, or a cabinet knob or wallpaper pattern that catches your fancy. Take notes and look for tendencies and consistencies in your choices.

Use the same technique when you look at showroom displays and manufacturers' brochures. What appeals to you? Warm and cozy? Cool and sleek? Light and airy? The answers will help you to decide what elements you want to work with in your design. For instance, if you like soft, sculptural shapes you may prefer a pedestal sink; but if you like clean, uncluttered lines you will probably prefer a Euro-style vanity washbasin.

## Design Principles

How can you tie these elements together to create the overall look that you want to achieve? The secret is to follow the basic principles of all design—line, form, scale, pattern, texture, and color. Look over your photographs; try to see how these principles are applied. The exercise will spark your own creativity.

## Line

The edges, corners, and decorative features of all of the elements in the room create an abundance of lines. The bathroom will feel more integrated and harmonious if these elements align as much as possible. For instance, the top of a doorway creates a horizontal line. If there is a window or a tall cabinet in the room, the design will be smoother if the top edge lines up with the top of the door molding. When it is impossible to position elements so that the edges are aligned, you can still create a unified feeling by introducing a line of tile or a strip of molding to tie the elements together.

Line also contributes to the feeling of a room. Strong horizontal lines emphasize serenity and make a bathroom feel more contemporary. Vertical lines emphasize formality and a traditional style. A narrow room will feel wider if lines cross the narrow dimension. You can achieve this effect by putting beams on the ceiling or a soffit across the top of the narrow wall. Diagonal lines add drama and movement; curves add elegance and grace to the room.

## Form

The principle of form relates to the shape and structure of the various elements in the design. Continuity in form also lends harmony to a design. Rectangular forms dominate most bathrooms, but in order to be harmonious, their proportions must be similar. Look at the shapes of the doors, windows, shower stall, bathtub, vanity, and cabinets. Do they all repeat a similar form, or do they clash? Is there one unique shape—a curved window or an archway, for instance? If so, you may want to repeat this shape elsewhere to tie the design together. Try to imagine the shapes as sculptural forms. Do they create a sense of harmony and balance? Does a large form, such as the bathtub, call attention to itself? If so, you can make it a dramatic focal point; or you can use color and texture to tie it into the rest of the design; or you can subdue its impact by recessing it into an alcove or sinking it into the floor.

**Opposite:** *Understanding design principles helps when it comes to doing a bathroom layout. A narrow strip of contrasting tile running the length of the floor accentuates the line and makes this room look longer than it is.*

## Scale

The principle of scale—an expression of relative size—refers to the relationships among the various elements of the room. Properly scaled spaces are neither too large nor too small for the people who use them. When considering the proper scale for the bathroom, look at the size of the room and the sizes of the various fixtures and finishes. If the room feels cramped, look for fixtures that are smaller than standard, small tiles, and a delicately patterned curtain fabric. If the room feels large or has a large window that expands the vista, think big. Choose large patterns, large tiles, large mirrors, and large basins.

## Pattern

Defined as repeated shapes, pattern is also the ordered regularity of the elements in a design. Because bathrooms have such an abundance of straight lines and rectangles, patterns created by tiles, grids, parallel wood grain, and strip flooring are usually appropriate. In most bathrooms the goal is to strike a balance between too much of the same pattern and too many different ones. One approach is to reduce pattern to a bare minimum by using mostly plain materials, or by using a few homogeneous, fine-patterned materials. The other approach is to introduce materials with random patterns, such as flat-grained wood cabinets, wall coverings with floral designs, stacks of towels, and plants, to break up the potential monotony of too many rectangles.

## Texture

Most bathroom textures—the visual and tactile surface of all of the materials used—are smooth for durability and easy cleaning, but even smooth surfaces can vary. Consider the differences to the touch among polished wood, glazed tile, porcelain, and glass. Think about texture when you choose all of your materials. Do you want your bathroom to feel sleek and shiny? Or do you prefer softer, more natural finishes?

## Color

A powerful design element, color is more than mere decoration. Color can transform space and give it much of its character.

A color wheel is helpful for choosing a color scheme. This device looks like a rainbow pie cut into 12 segments. The primary colors—red, blue, and yellow—are placed on the wheel at points equidistant from one another. Each of the secondary colors—green, orange, and violet—is spaced halfway between the two primary colors that it is blended from. The remaining six segments are tertiary colors, created by blending one primary with one secondary color. They are red-orange, red-violet, blue-violet, blue-green, yellow-green, and yellow-orange. Each segment can be further divided into graduated intensities that range from light tints to deep shades, all of the same value. Another type of color wheel used by designers completes the color options by showing within each segment colors that are created by adding black, white, red, blue, or yellow to produce variations ranging from off-whites to browns.

Harmonious color schemes can be created by combining colors from the wheel in various ways. Choosing one or more intensities from the same segment produces a monochromatic scheme. Choosing colors from opposite poles of the wheel, such as red and green or blue and orange, produces a complementary scheme. Note that in this scheme one color is always a primary, and the other a secondary. A triad is produced by taking colors from three segments spaced equidistant from one another.

A split complementary is produced by taking one color from one segment and the other two colors from segments on each side of the segment opposite the first. Not all color schemes combine opposites. Choosing colors from two or more contiguous segments creates an analogous, or related, scheme. More complicated schemes involve four colors. A double complementary consists of two complementary colors and the colors adjacent to each one that are also complementary to each other. A quadratic scheme consists of colors from any four segments, as long as no two segments are adjacent.

Remember that you will seldom be working with the pure hues and bright intensities of a color wheel. With practice, however, you will learn to locate on the wheel the colors that you are working with. For instance, oak flooring that is sealed but not stained is usually yellow-orange to orange, so something blue to blue-violet would be complementary. Terra-cotta tiles are usually red-orange. The actual color of a green rug may range from a yellow tone to a blue tone.

Where do you start? If there are permanent materials already in the bathroom, such as a mint green tile floor or a blue bathtub, start with that color and build a scheme around it. If you have carte blanche, start with tiles or a plumbing fixture or flooring material that you have already chosen, or with the colors in an adjacent room. You can also build a color scheme around a fabric or a wallcovering or a painting that you want to include in the bathroom.

Consider too the physical effects that colors produce. Reds, oranges, and yellows are warm; blues, greens, and violets are cold. Colors also have emotional value. Blue aids concentration. Green is peaceful and soothing. Red is stimulating.

Finally, you can use color to alter the spatial characteristics of the room. If the bathroom is small, use light colors to make it feel more spacious. If the ceiling is low, a light color will cause it to recede. If it is high and makes the bathroom feel too formal, use dark colors on the floor and countertops to create a more intimate feeling. Make a long, narrow bathroom feel wider by using light colors on the long walls and a dark color on the short end wall. Use intense colors to emphasize certain features, and pale colors to play them down.

## Choosing a Color

You should be aware of color terminology if you are going to discuss color possibilities with a designer. *Hue* refers to a color by name—red, blue, green, mauve. *Value* defines the relative darkness or lightness of the hue. Colors of lower value are dark, those of higher value are pale. *Chroma* defines the saturation of color. Strong chroma means a color that is rich and full. Weak chroma means a color with a flat look.

Consider these guidelines when you are deciding on a color.

☐ Ignore the name of the color; it can influence you more than you think.

☐ If you know you want a certain color, consider the full range of that color and think about combining different shades.

☐ Pay attention to an immediate response to a particular color. That impulse indicates your emotional preference.

☐ Narrow down your choices to three or four.

☐ Borrow or buy samples of each finish material (paint, tile, colored fixtures, wallcovering, fabric) and take them home with you.

☐ Remove as many colors as possible from the existing space (put drop cloths over surfaces that can't be removed).

☐ Place the samples in the room in which they will be installed. Look at the colors in various areas of the room, under various lighting conditions, and at various times of the day. Artificial light will change the appearance. Incandescent light adds a pinkish tone. Depending on the particular tube, fluorescent light may change the hue completely.

☐ As you decide on the colors you want, keep the paint chips and samples of the tile, wallcoverings, and flooring materials that you will be using. Attach everything to a sample board and keep it handy to refer to as you choose your other materials.

## A Brief Encyclopedia of Styles

It isn't easy to pin exact labels on bathroom styles. Most bathrooms are actually hybrids of several styles, or more often the unique and personal expression of the designer. This list is by no means definitive, but you may find it useful, in identifying your own style, to be aware of the following basic bathroom styles.

*Classical.* Designed on a grand scale reminiscent of Roman baths, these rooms feature an extensive use of marble or other dimensioned stone. This style is usually best used in an expansive space. Fixtures can be large and dominate including oversized whirlpool bathtubs, pedestal sinks, and both a toilet and bidet. Consider gold-colored fittings and other accents. Decoration may include a mural, decorative columns, pediments, statuary, and other references to antiquities.

*Modern.* Functional simplicity is the key to a modern bathroom. This style features flat surfaces, right angles, and severe lines. Use machine age materials, such as glass block walls; high-gloss, ceramic tile bathtub surrounds; brushed metal plumbing fixtures; and rubber tile flooring. Provide plenty of light. Decorations might be highly graphic, such as framed poster art and even neon sculpture.

*Victorian.* These sumptuous rooms offer a frenzy of floral fabrics and hand-painted accents and are a good style to choose for an older home. Consider fixtures that are more reminiscent of furniture than of equipment from a science lab. A claw-foot tub is well suited to this bathroom style as are free-standing washstands and antique dressers. Ceramic tile or vinyl products that mimic ceramic tile work well for finish surfaces. Cover windows with colorful curtains or white-painted shutters. Decorations can vary from botanical prints to old family photographs to doll collections.

*Art noveau.* A fanciful and exuberant display of organic forms with a sculptural feeling provides a room of ovals and curved lines that is modern without being harsh. Look for fixtures in curved form. Finish treatments can be plain ceramic or dimensioned-stone tile, usually in dark colors. Accents might continue the curved feel by featuring seashell or flower patterns.

*Art deco.* Glamorous bathrooms reminiscent of a Hollywood dressing room in the 1930s consist of abstract geometric forms, bright colors, multiple mirrors, glass shelves that seem to float, and a distinctive use of ceramic tile. A well-lighted vanity is a must for this style. Movie posters, tropical print curtains, and large plants complete this theme.

*Natural.* Bathrooms with an earthy, rustic feeling are considered natural style. Often these rooms have an indoor garden feel. Use wood, concrete, or stucco to create sculpted, handmade forms and keep colors muted. These rooms should be uncluttered, yet interesting to look at. Fixtures should be functional and blend into the room. Keep pipes covered, use recessed lighting, and play down plumbing fixtures. Finish treatments include slate tile, stone, and wood. Decorations might feature African or South American tribal art or framed museum prints.

*Oriental.* Austere but comfortable, oriental baths may feature a large soaking tub reminiscent of a Japanese bathhouse. These rooms make elegant use of natural materials, especially stone and wood. Keep basic colors muted and add bright accents that might change seasonally. A grid pattern—exemplified by shoji screens—provides the correct perspective for this type of room. This style of bathroom is well suited to coordination with an oriental garden that can be viewed from the room.

# BATHROOM LAYOUT

*O*nce you have surveyed the present bathroom, gathered ideas for the new design, and chosen an overall style, you will be bursting with ideas. Now you will want to make some sketches to begin designing your new room.

Begin by drawing a few preliminary floor plans and experimenting with different layouts. Use the floor plan of the existing bathroom, drawn to scale, as a start. Simply lay a sheet of tracing paper over it and sketch your new ideas on that. Make as many different tracings as you need. Or make several photocopies of the existing floor plan and sketch your ideas directly onto those. You can use these photocopies throughout the design process.

First position the major fixtures—toilet, bathtub, and shower. Try keeping them where they are. If this doesn't work or if you plan to use larger fixtures than the present ones (a luxury bathtub, for instance), start from scratch. If possible, find out exactly where you can rough in new drainpipes and vent pipes for the tub, toilet, and shower. Then concentrate on these locations for the major fixtures as you try new layouts. Don't worry about extending the water

supply pipes; they can be run almost anywhere the drainpipes can go.

To avoid having to sketch a new floor plan each time you try out a new idea, draw templates of the main elements to scale and cut them out. Then you can simply move them around on an open floor plan until you find a layout that works. Include the main plumbing fixtures—toilet, bathtub, shower, and washbasin—and any storage units that you know you will be using. Refer to the manufacturer's specifications for exact dimensions.

When you are juggling so many variables, it is easy to make a simple

error that defeats the entire scheme. Give yourself several weeks to complete this process. Don't commit yourself to one particular layout until you have experimented with all of the possibilities. Take some chances. Have fun. If a wonderful notion pops into your head when you're cooking, driving to work, or lounging in the tub, make a note of it and try it out. Albert Einstein once said that he got some of his best ideas while shaving. The important thing is to define the problems. Then let the solutions come of their own accord while you are doing other things.

*If you are remodeling, don't limit the available space to the existing bathroom. This double-sink countertop and dressing area was once a closet. By switching the closet area and the vanity area within the master suite, these homeowners gained natural light over their washbasins.*

# Drawing Plans

Many of your initial ideas will be simple sketches on napkins and paper scraps, but sooner or later you will need an accurate floor plan in order to proceed with designing your bathroom.

To make these plans you will need several inexpensive items. Most you will have around the house, others can be purchased at any hardware, stationery, or art supply store.

☐ A steel tape measure
☐ A ruler or a T square
☐ A pad of ¼-inch graph paper (four squares to the inch)
☐ Several pencils and erasers
☐ Tracing paper
☐ Masking tape
☐ A plastic right triangle
☐ A compass
☐ A plastic template of bathroom elements (optional)

The first step in plan drawing is to draw a base plan, an indication of permanent fixtures. A comfortable scale for drawing floor plans on graph paper is ½ inch (two squares) to 1 foot. Take exact measurements, accurate within ⅛ inch, and record them in feet and inches.

## Base Plan

Begin your base plan by measuring and recording the overall dimensions of the room. Then, add the dimensions of adjacent areas that the bathroom might expand into; the length of the wall space between windows, doors, and corners (measure to the window jambs and doorjambs, not to the edge of the trim); the width of the windows and doors (jamb to jamb); and the thickness of the walls. Draw walls with two parallel lines, the distance between them indicating the thickness of the wall. Shade in the walls to make them easier to see. Indicate windows with a third parallel line between the two wall lines. Show in which direction the doors swing.

The next step is to measure and indicate the location, width, and depth of each of the fixtures and cabinets that will remain in place. The plastic template will have samples for common bathroom fixtures.

To complete the base plan, mark the location of the heater, plumbing hookups, electrical outlets, and fan; the location of any steps or other changes in the floor height; and the location of overhead features, such as a skylight, low stairs, beams, or duct work. Use broken lines to indicate overhead beams and skylights. Use standard electrical symbols for lights, switches, and outlets.

Trace or photocopy this base plan so that you have several copies. During the course of designing your bathroom, you'll want to experiment with location options for all of your fixtures. Having several base plan copies will allow for convenient experimentation.

## Preliminary Plans

Use your base plan as a jumping-off point for designing your new bathroom. Determining preliminary plans, also called bubble diagrams, is a process of roughly drawing in various bathroom use areas onto copies of your base plan until you are happy with the results. Although you may be satisfied with your first effort, try several different designs to be sure that everything fits together well. Do not worry too much about exact dimensions as you play with the designs. Think now about relationships between elements and how you want the room to look.

Experiment with different options, moving fixtures to various sites within the room, expanding the bathroom into adjacent areas, and using different size fixtures to accommodate all your bathroom needs. This process is called refining the design. Many of the choices of bathroom layout will be determined by decisions of fixtures and finishes. Refining the design in discussed in the second chapter of this book. You should continue your preliminary plan experimentations as you make the choices discussed there. See page 58 for a discussion of how to avoid common mistakes when refining your design.

## Final Plan

Once you are happy with a particular preliminary plan, you need to make sure the dimensions will actually work within your room. Take a clean copy of your base plan and indicate the exact locations of all fixtures, cabinets, electrical outlets, and other built-in items. Measure carefully. Use the manufacturer's brochures for the exact dimensions of any fixtures or cabinets you have ordered but have yet to receive. When they are delivered, be sure to verify that they are exactly the size you expected.

Be sure to indicate any new water and sewer lines and changes in electrical and telephone lines on your final plan.

You may need to make several copies of the final plan for your local building department, inspectors, and workers. If you are remodeling and have a file of the architectural plans of your house, you should attach these drawings to this file, especially if utility lines will be affected.

## Elevation Drawings

After you have completed the final floor plan, make elevation drawings of the walls. Use a separate sheet of paper for each wall and label them north, south, east, and west. You can use the floor plan dimensions to get started and complete the elevations by taking field measurements as you go. Include doors, fixtures, shelves, and other major features of the room but do not include anything that you plan to get rid of. If you're not sure, however, draw it in. You needn't bother drawing in hardware and other fine details, except to experiment with options.

## Types of Bathrooms

Bathrooms can vary from a tiny half bath tucked away in a closet to a grand bathing suite the size of a common living room. Such variations in size, as well as in shape and function create almost endless possibilities when it comes to layouts.

The layouts presented here illustrate how various types of bathrooms can be arranged in rooms of different sizes and shapes. None of these bathrooms may suit your needs exactly, but they should give you a quick idea of how fixtures can be arranged in a given space.

### Powder Room

A powder room, or half bath, usually consists of a toilet and washbasin and is located near the areas of the home where visitors gather. Powder rooms tend to be small because space in these areas tends to be limited, but they need not be small if you have room to expand. A powder room slightly larger than usual gives a sense of extravagance and luxury that you may not be able to achieve anywhere else in the home. Because they are small and are frequented by guests, powder rooms are often

*Sample Powder Room Layouts*

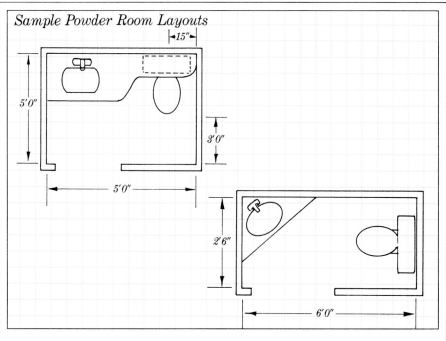

finished in finer materials than would be economical for larger bathrooms.

### Family Bathrooms

The layout of the family bathroom offers the greatest variety of options. This room must meet the needs of every member of the household, and sometimes these needs conflict. The need for privacy may conflict with the need for several people to use the

bathroom at once, or the need to store personal things in the bathroom may conflict with the need to make it available to guests. If the present bathroom is large enough, you may be able to solve the privacy problem by transforming part of it into a separate half bath, or by compartmentalizing it so that several people can use the room at the same time.

### Multiple-Entry Bathroom

A bathroom with more than one entrance, from a hallway and a bedroom, for example, or from more than one bedroom, allows for greater access—but at a price. Although the doorway itself takes up relatively little space, each entrance becomes a major element in the design when you consider the space required for the doorswing and access to the door as well as the loss of valuable wall space. Multiple entrances compound the problem by creating traffic corridors that divide and shrink the available space. If you cannot or do not wish to eliminate one of the doorways, consider moving it to improve the flow of traffic and free up congested space. You might also consider installing pocket doors, which take up less space than standard ones.

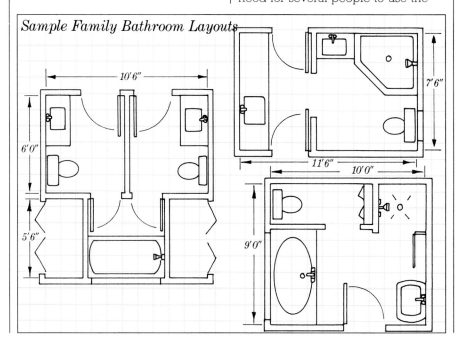

*Sample Family Bathroom Layouts*

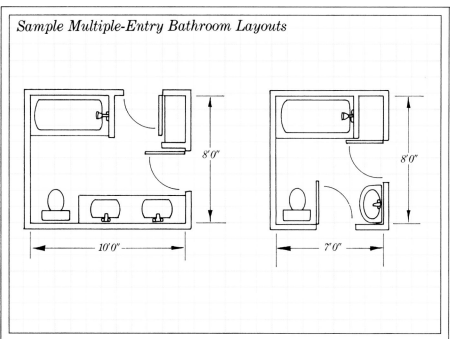

## Master Bathroom

Master bathrooms offer the greatest opportunity for a homeowner's personal expression as these rooms are rarely seen by guests and even other family members. Master bathrooms are private retreats that lend themselves to luxurious amenities and creative planning. Some are modest baths, placed next to the bedroom for convenience. Others are large suites that may include a dressing room, one or more closets, a sitting area, and an exercise area.

The master bathroom may consist of complete, separate his-and-hers bathrooms. If you are considering separate his-and-hers bathrooms, you may want to divide some of the facilities between the two areas. Consider, for example, a large shower and no bathtub in one bathroom and a whirlpool tub sans shower in the other.

Large or small, the master bathroom may be the only part of the house where the adult family members can have some privacy, and special care should be given to this important aspect of adult life.

## Open-Style Bathroom

An open bathroom is a highly personal space that forms part of a larger bedroom or suite. The centerpiece is usually a large soaking tub, and the toilet, bidet, and shower are compartmentalized. This type of bathroom takes special planning to ensure that the various spaces relate well to one another as well as to the larger room.

## Enlarging the Space

If the existing space is simply too small—as most older bathrooms are—now is the time to look for ways to expand. First see if anything can be moved out of the bathroom to create more space. If you want two separate washbasins, consider installing one of them in an adjacent bedroom. Place it on the common wall between the bedroom and the bathroom to make the plumbing easier. If a large storage unit or cabinet takes up valuable space, consider other storage options. Perhaps you could build shelves or soffit cabinets near the ceiling, install a high cabinet above the toilet, or recess narrow shelves into a wall.

You may be able to annex new space for the bathroom from adjacent areas. Are there any closets, dead-end hallways, unused rooms, or storage areas that the bathroom could expand into? If the bathroom has two or more entrances, could one of them be closed off? Does the bathroom have a separate entry area that could be better utilized by moving the door closer to the hallway? Are there places for recessed storage shelves within the wall cavities, or places

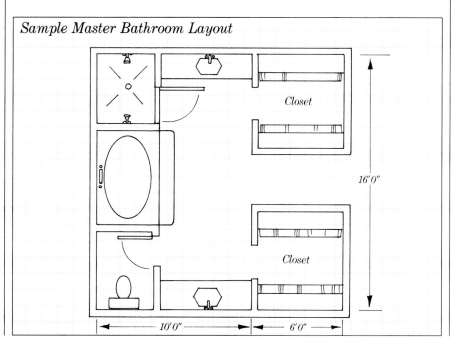

*Sample Master Bathroom Layout*

where cabinets or shelves could be set back so that they extend through the wall into an adjacent room?

A more drastic solution is to carve a completely new bathroom out of some other space in the house. Perhaps there is an office or a den that is underutilized, or a bedroom that is far too large. The old bathroom could then be used as a powder room, or the two spaces could be switched so that the old bathroom becomes a new, small den. Consider this solution if you are planning to gut the old bathroom and remodel it completely anyway.

If budget and space allow, you can always expand the bathroom outward. Some additions are modest bump-outs that cantilever beyond the existing foundation without requiring a new foundation of their own. Others are major annexes that include a complete bathing suite. One popular type of bathroom addition is a prefabricated sun space, often enclosing a luxury whirlpool spa.

Even if there is no way to add new space to the bathroom, there are ways to make it feel larger.

☐ Install a large picture window or a garden window, or even a glass door that opens on a private patio.

☐ Use shallow cabinets instead of standard 12-inch-deep cabinets.

☐ Use a large mirror to double the apparent space (but be careful—too much mirror, or too many mirrors, can be disconcerting).

☐ Use wall-mounted vanities or storage units so that the floor is visible beneath them.

☐ Exchange the vanity and washbasin for a pedestal or wall-mounted sink to add floor space.

☐ Use clear glass or clear curtains for the tub and shower enclosures.

☐ Add a skylight.

☐ Raise the ceiling.

☐ Use light, neutral colors throughout the space.

☐ Lower a wall so that it does not reach all the way to the ceiling, creating what is known as a pony wall.

☐ Change the direction of the doorswing (but avoid swinging it into a hallway) or install a pocket door instead. (Just remember that a pocket door requires substantial alterations in the framing, and there can be no plumbing or wiring in the wall cavity next to the door.)

## Minimum Clearances

In planning a bathroom layout, know what minimum clearances are required between the various plumbing fixtures. In a design where fractions of an inch count, it may be tempting to squeeze the fixtures too close together so that everything fits, but you must maintain the minimum clearances for safety and comfort. Your local building inspection department can give you the code requirements for your area, but the following guidelines are typical of most model codes. Remember that these are *minimum* standards. They do not guarantee that the bathroom won't feel cramped. Always try to allow more space than the code requires.

You'll find accessorizing easier and less expensive if your layout allows for standard size rugs, towel bars, shower doors, mirrors, and window treatments.

### Toilet

Allow at least 15 inches from the centerline of the toilet to a wall or bathtub on the side. A toilet compartment, therefore, must be at least 30 inches wide between finish walls, but 36 inches is better. If there is a washbasin beside the toilet, there should be at least 4 inches of clearance between the two fixtures. There also should be at least 21 inches of free space in front of the toilet, but 24 inches is more realistic.

Provide the same amount of space for a bidet as for a toilet. Because bidets are usually installed adjacent to toilets, be especially careful of the space between the two fixtures. Allow at least 15 inches of clearance between the two bowls, and be careful that you have allowed enough space for the comfortable use of each.

### Washbasin

There should be at least 21 inches of clearance—preferably 24 inches—in front of a washbasin. If the washbasin is beside a bathtub, allow at least 6 inches between the two fixtures.

### Shower Stall

Shapes and dimensions vary, but the floor of the shower pan should be large enough to contain a disc 34 inches in diameter. In addition, there should be at least 24 inches of clearance in front of the opening for stepping in and out.

### Bathtub

Allow enough space in front of the tub to get in and out easily. Also consider space for an adult to stand when helping a bathing child. Think, too, about standard bath mat sizes and allow enough sace in front of the tub for a good-sized rug.

If you are planning to use a prefabricated shower or bathtub surround, be sure to get the dimensions and clearances from the manufacturer. Side clearances for bathtubs vary, but do keep in mind space for doors, curtains and rods, or a wing wall to block shower spray.

**Opposite:** *Bathtubs come in a variety of lengths and widths, so consider all the options before you complete the bathroom layout. Here, the tub faucets were placed at countertop height, which left room for a slightly longer tub and a solid line of countertop along the back wall of this family bathroom.*

# REFINING THE DESIGN

D esign is a give-and-take process. It requires you to balance specific details of fixtures, fittings, and furnishings with the overall style you desire. This chapter will help you to refine the design of the new bathroom, using the preliminary layout as a starting point. Be prepared to change the layout as you get new ideas. It is useful to start with the major elements, but this is not really essential because all of the elements of a design are interrelated. Consider the plumbing fixtures, vanities, countertops, and storage systems. Consider, too, any special amenities that you want to add. All of these details must be thought out at the planning stage. Next consider the surface materials and the lighting and venting requirements. Keep in mind as you choose fixtures and finishes that these should harmonize with the accessories. Also consider whether the layout renders the new bathroom safe before you put your floor plan into final form. Try to give the same attention to all the small details of the room that you give to the major elements. Well-defined details can make the difference between a satisfactory bathroom and a stunningly beautiful showcase.

*An atrium on the other side of the glass-block wall and the bird-motif stained-glass window provide a tropical accent to this ladies bath. They can be seen from the whirlpool bath, as can the TV, which conveniently rolls back into the cupboard when not in use. For safety's sake, be sure to use a battery-operated remote control on electronic equipment while bathing. See page 32 for another view of this room.*

# PLANNING PLUMBING FIXTURES

There are many factors to consider as you plan each individual plumbing fixture. The most obvious are location, size, type, style, color, and material, but you should also consider special design features, convenience factors, and plumbing access.

Consider, too, whether the fixtures should function as a coordinated ensemble or as individual pieces. Manufacturers have always offered lines of fixtures in matching colors and styles, but some manufacturers also offer fixtures in colors that are meant to be mixed and matched. Some manufacturers have expanded the concept of a coordinated collection to include all the bathroom fittings and accessories, not just the plumbing fixtures. These lines include matching or coordinated faucets, sinks, towel bars, toilet paper holders, tissue holders, and waste baskets. Whatever your preference, the following information will help you to consider the design factors pertinent to each individual fixture.

## Bathtub

Few things in a house are more permanent than the bathtub. It cannot easily be moved or replaced, so you'll be making choices about its location, style, and color that you'll have to live with for a long time. In choosing the location, consider first the practical issues of access and plumbing. The tub should be convenient, but it should not impede the flow of traffic. It should be easy to get into and out of. If you are locating the faucet and spout on an exterior wall, make sure that the local plumbing codes allow it—some codes prohibit

pipes in exterior walls for reasons of energy conservation or accessibility. There should be a small door or removable panel on the backside of the end wall to provide access to the drainpipes and overflow pipes. The tub or shower valve can usually be reached through the front cover plate. If you want to locate the tub where it is impossible to rough in a new drain under the floor, you can raise the tub on a platform or get a special tub with a raised bottom. The drainpipe and P-trap can be installed above floor level in an adjacent wall.

Design factors also influence location. The bathtub is usually the most prominent feature of a bathroom. You can emphasize it even more by making it the focal point as seen from the entry, placing it in front of a large window, setting it into a large platform, or even pulling it out into the center of the room. If you want to make the tub less prominent, set it into an alcove or a corner.

Consider emotional factors and your own bathing habits. Do you enjoy bathing in the open, perhaps in the center of a luxurious suite or next to a window overlooking a panoramic view or a private garden? Or do you prefer an intimate, enclosed feeling, protected from outside distractions?

Other factors to consider are convenience to dressing areas and structural support for a heavy tub. Most residential floors are designed to carry 40 pounds per square foot. A 6-foot by 3-foot tub distributes its weight over 18 square feet. If the tub weighs 150 pounds, is filled with 60 gallons (about 500 pounds) of water, and contains two bathers whose average weight is 150 pounds, the total load will be 950 pounds, or 53 pounds per square foot. A cast-iron tub weighs much more, and some tubs hold more water. There are many variables that offset the weight of the tub, such as proximity to a bearing wall. Get professional advice about the need to reinforce the floor if you plan to install a large bathtub.

### Size and Type

Although bathtubs are available in many sizes and shapes, the standard tub is 5 feet long, 30 inches wide, and 14 to 16 inches high. It has a finish skirt on only one side and is meant to be installed between two end walls. It comes with the drain on the left or right. Tubs 4½-feet and 5½-feet long are also available in standard width.

Bathtubs made of new lightweight materials—acrylics reinforced with fiberglass—are available in a variety of shapes and sizes. Some have skirts, but most have unfinished sides and are intended for platform installation. Typical outside dimensions are approximately 5 feet long by 36, 40, 42, 44, or 48 inches wide; 5½ feet long by 30 or 36 inches wide; and 6 feet long by 33, 36, 42, 48, 56, or 60 inches wide. There are also spa-sized units for family bathing. Get exact dimensions from the supplier or from the manufacturer's specifications.

Do not rely on the outside dimensions of bathtubs for comparing sizes. The size of the interior bathing space is what counts. Two tubs may have the same outside dimensions, but the width of the rim, depth of the bathing space, angle of the sides, and water capacity may differ greatly. If possible, compare bathtubs by sitting in them, especially if more than one person will be using the tub.

Corner tubs can be installed where there is not enough wall space for a standard tub. The bathing area, which is positioned diagonally, is standard size, and the tub feels less cramped than a standard tub because there is a wide shelf in the corner. Traditional cast-iron tubs measure 4 feet or less along each side. In acrylic models each side usually measures 48 to 55 inches.

If you like the charm and playful whimsy of an old-fashioned claw-foot tub, you can buy a modern replica or have an original tub refinished. Faucets and fittings for an old tub may be found through renovator supply catalogs or specialty outlets.

## Material and Color

Enameled cast-iron bathtubs are the most durable and come in a wide array of colors. They feel solid, retain heat quite well, cushion sounds, and resist stains. They are also heavy; the bathroom floor may require structural reinforcement to take the larger sizes. Enameled steel tubs are less expensive than cast-iron ones, but they chip easily, can sound tinny, and come in a limited choice of colors. Bathtubs made of acrylic and fiberglass offer the widest choice of sizes and shapes. They are lightweight and hold heat better than tubs made of other materials. They come in deep and high-gloss colors as well as in standard colors and in white. They are easily drilled for custom faucet installations. The quality and durability of the finish have improved since fiberglass products first came on the market, and with proper care the new tubs will resist stains and scratches fairly well. Cast polymer tubs are also available and offer many of these same features. Even real marble is used for bathtubs. It is covered with layers of clear acrylic for durability. A custom-made tub of ceramic tile is another option. These Roman tubs look magnificent, but the flat planes and square edges characteristic of most tiling render them uncomfortable for long, relaxing baths. This problem can be solved by using small mosaic tiles that can be applied over curved surfaces to create a more contoured, comfortable shape.

Colors follow fashion trends, but a bathroom is a wonderful place for you to follow your own whims and express your own personal style. You may prefer a white bathtub because it is classic and never goes out of date, or a bone or almond bathtub because it suggests more warmth. Dark colors, such as navy blue or deep raspberry, and especially black, are very sensual but are also harder to maintain. A bright red or yellow creates a bold accent. Grays and pastels suggest refined elegance; and blues, greens, and marine colors are always appropriate around water. Of course, your choice of color will depend primarily on the overall color scheme of the bathroom.

Before you choose a new tub, consider keeping the old one. An enameled cast-iron bathtub in good condition is certainly worth keeping if you are satisfied with it. By changing the faucet, retiling the tub enclosure (or refinishing it with marble or solid surface material), and adding gleaming new doors or a stylish shower curtain, you can make an old fixture look as handsome as a new one. You may even prefer the elegant styling of the old tub to more modern designs. Even a cast-iron tub that is rust stained and worn can be professionally refinished, in place, with a new surface that will last for years.

## Special Features

Although bathtubs haven't quite reached the point of having power steering and cruise control, they offer many special features. One popular option is a whirlpool system. Water is pumped from the tub, mixed with air, and forced back into the tub through jets. This system is intended more for massaging than for cleansing, so a separate shower is convenient for washing up before or after the soak. Whirlpool systems are available with one-person, two-person, or larger tubs, so decide how many people will be using it when you choose the tub size. Unlike a spa, which has a filtering and heating system, a whirlpool bath is drained after each use. You will have a choice of jets—either a few large jets that produce a soft, soothing bath or several small, high-pressure jets that produce a forceful current for a stimulating massage. The motor is mounted at one end of the tub and must be accessible for servicing. Plan an access door, either at the end of the tub or in the side, as specified by the manufacturer. The whirlpool should have a safety switch for turning it on and off while you are in the tub. You should also consider whether the hot-water system has the capacity to fill the tub quickly. A 50-gallon hot-water tank is usually adequate, but check with a local plumber or the whirlpool supplier. You should also consult with your doctor if anyone in the family has special health problems that should be considered when you purchase this option. Finally, be sure that you are getting a whirlpool for the right reasons. It may be that what you want is a large, comfortable tub for long, hot baths and not necessarily the massage action. If so, you can get a large luxury tub without the expensive whirlpool feature.

Other options for a bathtub include a nonskid bottom, grab bars, pillows, a built-in sound system, and integral sides that eliminate the need for a waterproof enclosure.

## Faucet and Spout

It is not always necessary to wall-mount the faucet at the drain end of the tub. On platform tubs and tubs that are designed so that two people can recline at opposite ends, the faucet and spout should be mounted elsewhere. In planning the location, consider whether the handles are easy to reach, whether the spout interferes with reclining, and whether the handles or spout are in the way when you get into the tub. For platform tubs, decide whether the spout and faucet will be mounted on the deck or on the rim of the tub itself (which requires drilling holes in the rim). Some bathtubs have the filler spout built into the side of the tub. For these tubs a special vacuum breaker device must be installed in the water supply pipes to prevent the tub water from backing up into the system if the water pressure drops. The vacuum breaker must be located above the flood level of the tub, and it must be accessible for servicing. Some manufacturers provide a vacuum breaker with the tub. In addition to choosing the location, you will also have to choose the style of faucet you want and any special features, such as a telephone sprayer.

### Additional Amenities

Besides the bathtub itself, consider the area surrounding the bathtub. Are the floor surfaces skid-resistant? Will a step be needed to get out of the tub? A set of removable wood steps could be used to conceal whirlpool equipment. Are towel racks and towel storage convenient? Is there storage next to the tub for toiletries, reading material, eyeglasses, and so forth? Finally, is there adequate ventilation to prevent the buildup of steam and heat?

### Combination Tub-Shower

If the bathtub includes a shower, there must be some means of controlling the spray. Some tubs are large enough to contain the spray without an enclosure. Most tubs must have a shower curtain or sliding doors of tempered or safety glass. There are advantages and disadvantages to each system. Sliding glass doors feel permanent, but they also restrict access to the tub for cleaning it and for bathing youngsters. If you enjoy long soaks, you may find the glass doors claustrophobic because they leave only one side open. A shower curtain can be pushed all the way back for easier access and less confinement. As a design feature it helps to soften the hard surfaces and edges of the room, but it may also look temporary or create a cluttered effect.

Besides the doors or curtain, you have a choice of materials for the tub-shower enclosure. Tile is a traditional favorite, but marble, solid surface material, cast polymer, and other waterproof wallcoverings are also used.

### Shower

A separate shower stall is a high priority in most bathrooms today. Master bathroom suites are likely to have both a luxury bathtub and a walk-in shower stall. Some even have separate his-and-hers showers. Having both a tub and a shower enables two people to bathe simultaneously, allows a quick rinse before and after a hot bath, makes it unnecessary to step into the bathtub in order to take a shower, and eliminates the need for a shower door or a curtain on the tub. Finding room for a shower stall can be a problem if you are remodeling a small bathroom, however. Perhaps you can annex space from an adjacent closet. If there is not enough space for a shower and a tub, choose either a combination tub-shower or a shower stall with no tub at all.

*Decisions large and small must be made when you choose new bathroom fittings. For this child's bath, a dinosaur showerhead seemed most appropriate over the combination tub-shower. Note the beautiful ceramic tile that covers all the walls and floor of the room: There's green grass at the base, and there are clouds over the tub.*

A shower stall can go anywhere in the bathroom as long as you maintain the minimum clearance in front of the door (see page 22). When choosing a location, consider natural light, ventilation, access to towels, and access to a clear floor area for toweling off. Consider too how easy it will be for one person to use the other fixtures while another person is in the shower. Size may be a determining factor. The smallest practical size for a shower stall is 34 inches square on the inside dimension.

## Types

You can choose a prefabricated unit, a prefabricated shower pan with walls of tile or your choice of other material, or a completely custom-made shower stall. Prefabricated units are installed in much the same way as other plumbing fixtures. They come in a variety of shapes, sizes, and colors. Most are square or rectangular, with one open side for a doorway or two open sides, one to take a glass panel and one for a doorway. Corner units with a diagonal front, called neo-angle units, are also available, as are units with no threshold, for wheelchair use. Some luxury units have an optional top that converts them to steam rooms. Sizes range from 32-inch squares (not large enough to meet some local codes) to 36-inch by 48-inch rectangles. The most common material is fiberglass with a finish surface of acrylic or other plastic. All of these finishes require nonabrasive cleaners. The walls of the unit are not structural; they must be attached to rigid framing. No tiling is required. Some units have ceilings. Some have

doors, but for most models the door must be purchased separately. Some have molded seats, soap dishes, and ledges. Prefabricated units are quite easy to install. The most difficult problem is usually getting them into the bathroom because they are larger than a standard doorway. Some models come in two or more sections that can be assembled in place.

Prefabricated shower pans are molded from plastic, terrazzo, or similar

chipped stone. They enable you to choose walls of any material without having to order a custom-made waterproof shower pan. They can be used with prefabricated shower surrounds or custom materials, such as tile, marble, or solid surface slabs. The stone pans look and feel more substantial than most plastic or fiberglass pans. Some color options are available. Some models have skid-resistant floors, which can be

*Dual showerheads and an interesting tile treatment individualize this oversized stall shower in a gentleman's bath. Although the tiling looks complicated, it is actually just simple straight lines of black tile. The corner tiles have been cut at a diagonal and then matched with diagonally cut white tiles.*

difficult to clean. The range of sizes is usually wider for shower pans than for full prefabricated units. For ready-made showers the front curb is typically 4 inches and the edges 5 to 6 inches above the floor.

Custom-made shower stalls offer the most flexibility. They can be designed to match the available space, the bathing needs of the users, and the creative imagination of the designer. They do not all resemble closets or phone booths. Some are small rooms that have multiple shower heads and may double as steam rooms. Others are open stalls that have low walls so that they feel like part of the surrounding bathroom. Some have windows that look out on panoramic vistas. Some are circular, like seashells. The walls can be made of tile, marble, slabs of solid surface material, cast polymer, tempered glass, glass block, or anything else that is waterproof and easily maintained. The floor pan of a custom shower must be installed properly to keep it from leaking. This is usually best done by a professional plumber or tile setter.

Whatever type of stall you choose, you have design flexibility regarding the height of the walls and ceiling. If you prefer maximum closure, consider a lower ceiling, say 7 feet. Run the tile up to and across the ceiling to control moisture problems. If you like a more open feeling, build the enclosure walls only 6½ feet high, so that there is 18 inches of open space above them. A vaulted ceiling or a skylight that opens can be used to create dramatic effects over an otherwise standard shower stall.

## Doors and Side Panels

Prefabricated shower door units are available in many styles and configurations. For recessed stalls you will need only a door, with jambs and hardware for mounting it in the opening; for stalls with one or more open sides you can order fixed panels to match. These panels must be made of tempered glass, safety glass, wire glass, or plastic. You have a choice of clear, etched, or smoked glass. You can also individualize the glass by having a design etched into it or a stained glass overlay applied to it. The metal edge, or frame, holding the door and panels in place can be finished in chrome, brass, brushed gold, bronze, white, black, or a limited number of decorator colors. Frameless doors are also available.

Some doors are hinged along the edge. Others have pivots attached to the top and bottom to keep the doorswing at a minimum arc and to allow one edge of the door to close against the inside of the jamb for a tighter seal. Sliding doors are also available for wide openings. Most door and side panel assemblies are approximately 70 inches high.

*Clear tempered-glass shower doors let daylight into the bathroom. Use a glass cleaner available in automotive parts stores to keep the glass sparkling clean. The wood plank ceiling, the gray-stained wood trim on the solid surface-material countertop, and the slate tile floor combine to give this room a natural feeling.*

## Valve and Head

Selecting a shower valve and a showerhead is no longer a simple matter of choosing between a chrome finish and a brass finish. As you consider all the style and performance features that today's shower fittings offer, you might think you were buying an appliance, not a faucet. For instance, in selecting the handle action you have a choice between two separate handles and a single handle; in a single handle, you can choose among a knob, a lever, and a combination of both. Whatever your choice, you should visit a showroom where you can test different models to compare the action as well as the styling.

You have functional choices as well. Many shower valves include a control that keeps the water at an even temperature when someone runs water elsewhere in the house. This feature prevents you from scalding yourself accidentally; it is mandated by many local codes for new installations. There are two types of temperature control. A thermostatic control reads the temperature of the water and maintains it. A pressure-balancing control reads the incoming hot and cold water pressures and automatically adjusts to any fluctuations. Some valves have digital read-outs to tell you what the water temperature is. The working parts of faucets include sophisticated engineering and materials that make the valve work smoothly for many years.

Showerheads offer even more options, including water-saving features, massage sprays, flexible tubing for either hand-held or stationary operation, a wall bar for adjusting the height of the showerhead, and multiple heads for body spraying.

Finishes and styling range from traditional porcelain knobs to sleek Euro-style fittings in bold colors.

## Additional Amenities

Plan how you will store soap and other toiletries in the shower. Most prefabricated units have soap dishes and shelves molded into the walls. If you are tiling the walls, you can buy a soap dish that matches the tiles, or you can create alcoves and ledges for storing things. A bench is another amenity to consider. If there isn't enough room for a built-in bench, you might want a fold-down model that can be mounted on the wall. For lighting, the bathroom light fixture may be sufficient if it is close enough to the shower, but a light inside the shower is preferable. It should be rated for wet areas. Think about ventilation too. A ceiling fan may not be adequate unless it is close to the shower stall. Another good way to provide ventilation is to install a working skylight over the shower. Finally, plan grab bars that can be used by young and old alike.

*This bathroom and the one on the previous page share the same basic layout. Their different looks come from the differences in fixtures and finish materials.*

## Toilet

Depending on the floor plan and on matters of privacy, the toilet can be placed along a wall, in a shallow alcove, or in a compartment of its own. Most toilets measure approximately 27 inches out from the wall if they have a conventional rounded bowl and 30 inches if they have an elongated bowl. They are 20 to 24 inches wide. The height depends on whether the tank is separate or is incorporated into a low-profile, one-piece design. One-piece toilets are 19 to 20 inches high; two-piece toilets are 26 to 28 inches high.

### Functional Option

Like all plumbing fixtures, toilets offer many choices when it comes to performance. One important feature is water conservation. Most water-saving toilets use about 3.5 gallons per flush, but some states and the federal government have considered legislation to mandate flush rates as low as 1.6 gallons. A local supplier or the building inspection department can tell you what the current law requires. Unlike a conventional toilet with a brick or a dam placed in the storage tank, a water-saving toilet is specifically designed to produce a sanitary flush using a very small amount of water.

Noise is another consideration. Some toilets flush more quietly than others. Bear in mind too that hard surfaces, such as tile or marble, amplify any sound within the bathroom,

whereas plastic drainpipes and unsecured water pipes amplify the sound of rushing water and carry it throughout the house.

Other functional options include insulating liners to prevent water condensation on the toilet tank in hot or humid regions; an elongated bowl to suit a wider range of users; extrahigh models for users who are tall or who have limited mobility (the rim of these models is 18 inches above the floor instead of the standard 15 inches); and a reinforced seat with supporting arms for users who need extra grab bars. Wall-mounted models free up the floor space for easier cleaning and a less cluttered look. Like conventional toilets with a rear outlet, they solve the problem of roughing in a new toilet drain in a bathroom with a concrete slab floor. There are also special toilets that fit into corners.

### Style Options

Many people view the toilet as a necessary convenience and don't think very much about styling—they simply buy the cheapest model or reuse the old one. At most they may give some thought to color. You should consider, however, how the toilet fits into the overall design; it is just as important as any other feature. A prominently located toilet commands as much attention as a large sculpture. And, indeed, some manufacturers offer unique designs that are seriously meant to be (and can cost as much as) works of art.

In choosing a toilet, the main style options are size, shape, and color. A low, one-piece toilet will not be as prominent as a two-piece toilet and for that reason can fit into a wider range of design schemes. A two-piece,

*Bidets, common in the finer homes of the Victorian era and long popular in Europe, can once again be found in American bathrooms. A bidet is usually installed near a toilet.*

or tank, toilet has greater bulk and substance, which can be a benefit in some designs and a distraction in others. The shape and styling of the toilet must also be considered. These details give the toilet grace and form. Some toilets have emphatic angles and strong geometric shapes. Others have softer, more flowing lines. Some shapes and styles evoke a specific period. Examples are a copy of a Victorian tank toilet or a stepped, art deco design. Compare various models to see which one blends in the best with your particular design scheme.

When choosing color, as with bathtubs, consider the overall scheme. If you want the toilet to be subdued and unobtrusive, choose a neutral color that matches the floor or the surrounding walls. If you want to emphasize the sculptural lines of the fixture, choose white, light gray, or a pastel color. For a bold, whimsical statement, choose a bright color. Along with color, consider finish options for the handle. Most handles are available in chrome or brass, and some manufacturers offer a variety of colors and vintage designs. European models feature push buttons or pull knobs on the top of the tank. Choose the seat at the same time as you choose the toilet. Matching seats are available for most toilets, but you can select a different seat to create a contrast or to unify the toilet with other elements in the room—a wood seat to match the vanity, for example.

## Related Issues

When you select a toilet, verify the rough-in dimensions for the drain and the water supply valve. For most toilets the floor drain is centered 12 inches out from the finish wall. When verifying the location of the supply valve, check the measurements with the actual toilet or a showroom model. Manufacturers sometimes specify generic measurements, and you can modify them so that the supply tube rises gracefully toward the tank inlet without any unnecessary loops or kinks. (See page 102.)

A toilet is not a wastebasket or an ashtray; remove any temptation to use it as one by having these amenities near at hand. Otherwise, you are asking for plumbing problems.

## Bidet

Although bidets are not used as widely in the United States as they are in Europe, they are gaining popularity in the States. The fixture is designed for cleansing the perineal region of the body conveniently and comfortably without having to use the tub or shower and can be used by any member of the family. The user sits astride the bowl, facing the faucet. A bidet works like a washbasin. It can be filled with water from the faucet spout, but modern bidets also provide a flow of water around the rim to rinse it. Some offer the option of a continuous stream of water ascending from the center of the bowl.

Locate the bidet close to the toilet for convenient use. If the two fixtures are installed side by side, leave at least 15 inches between them. Check the local code to determine the required minimum clearance. Most plumbing codes also require a vacuum breaker in the water supply piping if there are any water inlets below the rim of the bidet.

*One solution to the problem of a shared bathroom is to compartmentalize its various functions. The pedestal sink is in the bedroom, and the toilet and shower each have a private room.*

## Washbasin

Although it is the smallest of the plumbing fixtures, the washbasin or lavatory is in some ways the center of bathroom activity. It is used more often than any other fixture, and it fills a variety of needs; it is equally suited to a quick washing up or to an elaborate grooming ritual.

### Type

The main decision to be made when planning a washbasin is whether it should be mounted in a countertop or standing as a separate fixture. A countertop installation has the advantage of providing a convenient work surface around the basin, and it makes the basin itself blend into the bathroom furnishings. Because a counter installation usually includes a vanity, it also provides extra storage space, concealed plumbing connections, and the extra flair that rich cabinetry and a glistening counter bring to the design. The main drawbacks to a vanity installation are the potential for clutter that the countertop presents and that the cabinet takes up space.

The alternative to a countertop installation is a freestanding basin, either a pedestal model, a wall-mounted model, or a revival of the traditional sink console. These basins are less bulky than a vanity. By exposing more of the floor and wall areas they make the room feel larger. They are three-dimensional, sculptural objects, with graceful lines and colorful, contoured surfaces. Some models have a distinctively modern look; others create a specific vintage effect—Victorian, Edwardian, or art deco. Models with a fluted pedestal are classical in feeling. The drawbacks to a free-standing installation are that some of the plumbing is exposed and the lack of countertop and storage space.

The location and number of washbasins are determined by the available space and by the needs of the users. There are several satisfactory ways to fit two washbasins into a bathroom. One is to use a long or L-shaped counter. If the basins are side by side, allow a minimum of 30 inches of counter for each basin (for a total of 5 feet). Another arrangement is to separate the basins, perhaps placing them back-to-back in a peninsula or island configuration, or on adjacent walls. Allow at least 3 feet of maneuvering space, with no overlap, in front of each basin. Another option is to move one basin into the dressing area or into a separate compartment outside the main bathroom in order to preserve privacy in both spaces. Finally, if there is no space in or near the bathroom itself, consider installing one of the basins in a bedroom.

Other factors that affect the location of the washbasin are ease of access from the bathroom entry; natural light from a window or skylight; and sufficient space for such amenities as a wall mirror, a medicine cabinet, electrical outlets, towel bars, and shelves or a cabinet for storage.

### Style

Washbasins are no longer simple round bowls with plumbing attached. They are as sophisticated and dazzling as furnishings designed for any room in the home, and they come in a stunning array of colors and styles. In selecting a basin, consider practical issues as well as your overall design. How much space is there for the basin? If it is mounted in the countertop, will the rim be above the counter, flush with it, or below it? What type of faucet will you use? What hole spacings does that type of faucet require? Are there any special uses to consider, such as bathing a baby? Are any of the users exceptionally tall? Will anyone need an extrawide bowl for washing forearms and elbows? Some wall-mounted basins can be adjusted to accommodate users with different needs.

There are many ways to fit a washbasin into the bathroom design. A basin with bold color and strong styling can be a focal point, whereas a simple, recessed bowl can seem to fade into the background. Whatever your preference, remember that color will have more effect on the design than either size or style.

You can use the following summary of size and shape options to plan the washbasin for your preliminary design. As soon as you have selected a basin, use the manufacturer's specifications to revise the rough plan.

### Size and Shape

Countertop washbasins can be round, oval, rectangular, or hexagonal. Round basins are usually 18 to 19 inches in diameter. Oval basins are 17 to 20 inches wide by 14 to 17 inches deep (front to back). Most rectangular basins are 20 to 22 inches wide by 17 to 19 inches deep, but they can be as much as 28 inches wide or as small as 11 inches by 11 inches. Hexagons are 20 to 22 inches wide by 16 to 19 inches deep.

Wall-mounted basins are rectangular. Most models are 19 to 20 inches wide by 17 to 18 inches deep. Smaller models are typically 16 inches wide by 12 inches deep.

Pedestal sinks, which are really wall-mounted basins with a decorative support, are 20 to 28 inches wide by 16 to 21 inches deep and 30 to 32 inches high.

Besides size and shape, consider the number and spacing of holes needed for the faucet. The options are no holes (the faucet is mounted on the countertop); a single hole for a single-post faucet; or three holes, with the outside holes centered 4 inches apart for standard faucets, and up to 16 inches apart for wide-set faucets.

### Material

Most washbasins are made of vitreous china. They are durable, easy to clean, and beautiful, although they can crack if something heavy is dropped on them. Enameled cast-iron basins are easy to clean and more durable than vitreous china but not as smooth. Pottery basins are made in limited production, typically in earth colors, and have the feeling of custom-made, one-of-a-kind pieces. The durability and surface smoothness of these basins depends on the glaze. Basins are also available in synthetic materials, often molded into countertops of the same substance. Cast polymer may have a gelcoat finish, or a clear finish, which may eventually wear away. Solid surface materials are more durable and come in several colors and styles, including faux granite. The least expensive basins are enameled pressed steel, which is lightweight, fairly durable, and easy to clean. Another lightweight option is provided by the new composite materials, such as epoxy and compressed quartz, which often come in bold, dramatic colors.

## Faucets

Fancy or plain, faucets are making a big splash in bathroom design. Many are so stylish that if you simply replaced all the faucets in your bathroom, it might look as if you had done a complete remodeling. Faucets are too small to be considered a focal point of the design; think of them as jewelry for the fixtures. It is not uncommon to spend more money on the faucet than on the fixture itself, and if you are investing in quality throughout the bathroom, you should not settle for cheap faucets. For tight budgets, it often makes better sense to choose an inexpensive fixture and then splurge on the best faucet you can possibly buy. As is true of bathroom design in general, many of the new styles and trends originate in Europe. However, American manufacturers offer both traditional and Euro-style faucets.

Most washbasin faucets have one spout for both hot and cold water; these are called mixers. In a center-set (or center-fit) faucet, the spout and handles are all in one unit. In a wide-set faucet, the spout and handles are separate and the connection between them is concealed below the deck. Center-set faucets can have either single or dual controls. On some

dual-control models the two handles are connected directly to the side of the spout; on others, the spout and handles are all connected to a small base. Most center-set faucets are designed for a standard three-hole basin, with the outside holes spaced at 4 inches, on center. Some have a single-post design that requires only one hole. (A matching escutcheon plate is usually available for covering up the other two holes if the mixer is mounted in a standard three-hole basin.)

Wide-set faucets offer flexibility of installation. They can be adapted to fit holes spaced anywhere from 4 to 16 inches apart, on center. They can be individualized even more if they are mounted in a countertop next to the sink. For example, the spout could be placed at a rear corner and the handles off to the side. This is handy for tight installations where there is no room for a full faucet along the back edge of the basin.

### Finish and Style

The bodies of almost all faucets are made out of brass, but they are covered with a variety of finishes. The traditional standard is chrome, which is very easy to maintain and holds up for years. Brass itself is also popular, in a bronze, antique matte, or highly polished finish. Brass tends to tarnish easily, so various protective coatings have been developed to preserve the original sheen. Most of these coatings are lacquers that do not hold up very well under the kind of use and abuse that faucets receive. Once they scratch or begin to peel off, the brass tarnishes rapidly. Recoating is difficult and seldom entirely satisfactory. More durable coatings, such as polymer resin, are generally worth the extra cost. In some cases the manufacturer leaves the finish off intentionally so that the brass will tarnish and achieve a soft patina with age. Of course, brass can always be kept shiny with regular polishing. Another option is gold plating, which has a certain cachet of its own and also resists tarnishing.

Colored faucets add a different kind of design excitement. Colors range from white or black to intense red or yellow, from subdued almond or gray to designer accents of teal or rose. Sometimes lacquers are used for the colored finish, but epoxy resins are more durable.

Other finish materials may be used in faucets for the handles or as accents. White porcelain or ceramic handles, in the familiar cross and lever styles, add a vintage look. Handles may also be made of wood or clear acrylic, or of onyx, crystal, or other semiprecious stones.

Faucet styles are as varied as the finishes. Selection is a matter of personal choice. Consider how well the faucet harmonizes with the rest of the bathroom design. Consider practical matters too. How high is the spout? How easy is it to turn the handles with wet or soapy hands? Do you want the spout to swivel? (If you do, a faucet for a bar or a kitchen sink may work nicely in the bathroom.)

### Internal Workings

Faucet mechanisms have advanced a long way beyond the simple valve stem with replaceable washers that wore out every few years (although such faucets are still sold). Precision metal parts, synthetic materials, and hard ceramics have made the washerless faucet commonplace, and on those rare occasions when maintenance is required, the repair is a simple matter of replacing a modular assembly. Ceramic disc faucets can go from *off* to full *on* in only a quarter turn of the handle.

### Accessories

Washbasin faucets normally include a pop-up drain assembly. In most cases the drain flange and stopper match the finish of the faucet, but check to be sure. Options available are a sprayer, a flexible spout, and a water-saving aerator. For a master bathroom you might also consider an instant hot-water tap for quick morning coffee or midnight toddy.

# PLANNING VANITY AREAS

T he area surrounding the vanity offers many opportunities in bathroom design. The vanity itself is the essence of practicality. It is an efficient cabinet for storage, for housing all of the plumbing connections, and for supporting a basin and countertop. At the same time, a unique vanity can transform a utilitarian bathroom into a pleasant living space.

In the midst of specialized plumbing fixtures and hard-finish surfaces, vanity areas should be treated as familiar furniture. If a vanity is long, taking up one whole wall of the bathroom, it sets a tone of relaxation and repose. If it has a wood finish or rounded edges that invite touching, it can offer a warm contrast to porcelain and tile. A traditional dressing table, which has no washbasin, invites the user to linger rather than to rush. On the other hand, the vanity can be a whimsical, unique creation, one that is meant to stimulate as well as soothe. The possibilities are almost limitless.

The vanity area is made up of washbasin and faucet, which were discussed as part of your utility decisions, the countertop, the medicine cabinet, and the mirrors. Lighting and electrical outlet needs will also play a part in determining the final look of your vanity area.

## Vanities

There should be enough room in front of the vanity for the doors and drawers to open and close without interference. There should be enough wall space for a mirror and lighting. If one or both sides of the vanity are exposed, allowing a corner to jut out into the center of the room, consider curved edges to minimize painful bumps. Determine exactly how much storage space you will need and plan spaces for specific items. If you are buying a modular unit, the size of the storage spaces will be predetermined, so make sure that they meet your needs. Whether you intend the vanity to be a striking centerpiece or a subdued background to other, more dramatic features of the bathroom, it should fit in with the overall design.

Consider related storage areas at the same time as you consider the vanity. Prefabricated, matching modular units, such as standard base or wall cabinets, drawer units, tall storage cabinets, and toppers to go over the toilet tank, are available from many manufacturers and can be used to create a coordinated ensemble.

## Type

You can buy a vanity as you would a modular kitchen cabinet, or you can have one custom-designed and built by a local cabinet shop. Like kitchen cabinets, vanities come in a wide array of materials, colors, and styles. Some resemble period pieces, others contemporary furniture. Vanities are often sold as a package with a countertop. These countertops are usually made of cast polymer or solid surface material and have the basin molded into them.

The standard front-to-back depth for a vanity is 18 to 21 inches. Widths start at 18 inches and continue in 6-inch increments to 72 inches. Matching filler can be used to adapt a standard vanity to fit any space. Most vanities are 29 to 30 inches high, including the countertop, but you can shim or trim the base to adjust the height for a specific user or for comfortable seating.

## Countertops

Bathroom counters are not confined to the vanity. They can cantilever out from the wall, or they can be extended beyond the vanity to create a larger, more useful surface. A "banjo" countertop covers the top of a vanity and continues in a graceful curve to become a narrow shelf over the adjacent toilet. A long, continuous countertop may connect two separate vanities, or it may extend beyond the vanity to become a window shelf.

### Materials

Countertops can be made from all sorts of materials; the range of colors, textures, and design possibilities is immense. If you want a countertop with a basin molded right into it, choose cast polymer or solid surface material. These basin-countertops are all one integrated, seamless unit. If you want a separate washbasin, choose from among plastic laminates, ceramic tile, marble, granite, and wood, as well as solid surface material.

Cast polymer countertops generally come with the basin already molded in. They are available in many pastel colors, and they are relatively inexpensive. Cast polymer is easy to clean, but because the finish surface is only a veneer, it is prone to damage from scorches, scratching, and wear, some of which can be repaired by buffing.

**Opposite:** *An L-shaped vanity area allows for a seating space separate from the washbasins. Consider all of the uses to which the vanity area will be put and make sure that you have allowed counter space and storage space for all of them.*

Solid surface material is more expensive than cultured marble, but it is much more durable because the color and texture are uniform throughout. It comes in a wide range of colors and designs, from soft white to designer colors to faux granite and marble. Stains, scratches, and burns can be removed with a light sanding. The solid surface material is available in plain slabs or in preformed basin-countertops. It is sold under such trademarks as Avonite, Corian, Fountainhead, and 2000X brands.

High-pressure plastic laminates are thin veneers of durable plastic material. They must be glued to a stable substrate, usually high-density particleboard. This can be done on the job site, at a cabinet shop, or at factories that produce postformed countertops. Laminates come in an almost unlimited range of colors, patterns, and textures. They are easy to clean and are generally the least expensive option, but they scorch and scratch easily, and they have brittle edges if they are not fabricated properly. Another problem arises with standard laminates that consist of a dark base layer covered by a very thin surface layer. The surface is attractive, but if the edge is exposed, which happens when two pieces of laminate are joined at right angles, it creates a dark, distracting line. There are two ways to solve this problem. One is to roll the laminate down over a curved countertop edge, eliminating the need for a separate trim piece. The other is to use a newer type of laminate that has solid color all the way through.

Ceramic tile is a traditional favorite for countertops. It too comes in a wide range of sizes, shapes, colors, and textures. It is durable and moderately expensive, and it lends itself to do-it-yourself installations. It can be individualized more easily than other countertop materials with the use of accent pieces or custom-made decorative tiles. The grout lines can be distracting in some bathroom designs and are also subject to mildew and staining unless they are treated properly. Ceramic tile countertops can be repaired by replacing only the damaged tile or tiles, unlike solid slabs or continuous-surface countertops. The most common sizes of tile for countertops are 3-inch and 4-inch squares and mosaics 1 to 2 inches in diameter. Many—but not all—tile patterns include matching edge pieces for trimming the front and sides of the countertop, cove pieces for the bottom of the back splash, and bullnose pieces for trimming around a recessed basin. Order trim pieces at the same time as you order the regular tiles so that you will be sure that they are available.

*It's the little details that make a house a home. The cabinet knobs and drawer pulls in this newly remodeled Southwestern-style bathroom are over 30 years old and have graced several of this family's other bathrooms. They are turquoise stone and match perfectly the rope accent tile along the vanity back splash and the shower surround.*

Slabs of marble or granite can be used for bathroom countertops. Granite is extremely durable. Marble, however, is easily stained and is particularly susceptible to anything acidic, such as chlorinated water. For this reason it should be sealed periodically. Both materials are also available as dimensioned-stone units, usually 12 inches square. They are installed in the same way as tile.

Wood must be used with extreme caution in a bathroom, especially for horizontal surfaces, such as countertops. Certain species—teak and redwood, for example—are more suitable than others, but all wood must be treated carefully and sealed properly to stand up under normal bathroom use.

### Trim and Details

Consider the trim and the back splash as you select the countertop material. The front and side edges are usually trimmed to match the countertop. The back splash can match, or it can be made of a different material altogether. For instance, decorative tile or glass block can be used as a back splash with plastic laminate, solid surface, and marble countertops as well as with tile ones. If you plan to install a large mirror on the wall behind the countertop, you may want to eliminate the back splash and extend the mirror all the way down to the counter. This will create a dramatic effect, but the mirror will be a little more likely to break and difficult to keep clean.

## Medicine Cabinet

The familiar medicine cabinet, beloved of TV commercials and get-well cards, serves many useful functions.

*Before determining your vanity area finish, decide on washbasin and faucet styles. This decision will affect some of your tile trim choices.*

It provides safe, convenient, eye-level storage for medicines; it is an easily accessible place to keep toiletries; and its door doubles as a handy mirror. However, these functions need not be combined in a single unit. You may prefer to install a large wall mirror in place of the medicine cabinet and store medicines and toiletries elsewhere. On the other hand, you could place a mirror and a medicine cabinet on adjacent sidewalls to create a mirrored corner.

Most medicine cabinets are designed to be recessed into the wall so that only the thickness of the mirror door protrudes. Surface-mounted cabinets are used where framing, insulation, pipes, ducts, or other obstacles make it impossible to install a recessed cabinet. They extend 4 to 6 inches out from the wall and have finished sides. Typical sizes

for a single-door cabinet are 15 to 18 inches wide by 26 to 36 inches high. Sizes for double- and triple-door units are typically 30, 36, or 48 inches wide by 26 or 34 to 36 inches high. Larger units may be 54, 60, 72, or 80 inches wide by 36 to 40 inches high.

You have many options when it comes to mirrors, doors, and shelves. Doors can be hinged or sliding. Most single doors can be reversed to open on the left or on the right. Some units are especially designed for corner installations. Others are designed to be installed as a pair with a wall mirror between them, to create an adjustable three-way mirror. Some units have three mirrors built into the cabinet. Most units have adjustable mirrors and shelves. Instead of a mirror you may prefer a wooden louvered door, or a favorite painting.

Medicine cabinets come frameless and in a wide choice of frames made of chrome, wood, brass, or colored metals. In many units a bar of bulb lights can be installed along the top of the cabinet.

Like all bathroom fixtures, medicine cabinets have entered the world of high style. The ultimate model is an elaborate console, 6 feet wide, with glamorous styling and rich materials. It may be equipped with multiple cabinets, drawers, and slide-out trays; electrical outlets on the inside; soft lighting, with dimmer controls, around the sides and top; smoked or etched mirrors; adjustable side mirrors; a lockable storage compartment for medicines; concealed hinges and hardware; and mirrors on both sides of the doors, so that you can see yourself whether the doors are open or shut.

In choosing a medicine cabinet, consider its dimensions and proportions in relation to the other features of the room. For example, if you are installing the medicine cabinet above a vanity and mounting a light bar over the top, all three fixtures should align smoothly and should be in proportion to one another. If the medicine cabinet is too small, it will be overwhelmed by the vanity; if it is too large, it will draw the eye away from the vanity, diminishing its impact.

## Mirrors

Not only do mirrors serve as aids to grooming, but they amplify the light in a room and constitute a strong design element as well. They affect one's perception of the space and, in the case of multiple mirrors, create interesting illusions that can work for or against the design. A small mirror in a medicine cabinet or a wardrobe mirror on a door has little or no effect on the design, but large expanses of mirror must be planned carefully. You can buy mirrors in standard sizes from a building supplier, or a glass shop will cut them to order and install them for you.

### Practical Considerations
When planning mirrors, consider the family's grooming needs first. The vanity or washbasin should have a mirror that is well lighted and at a convenient height for everybody who is going to use it. You may also want a second, magnifying mirror that can be adjusted to various stationary positions. Some of these mirrors are mounted on retractable arms, some on the back of the medicine cabinet door, and some on suction cups so that they can be kept in a drawer and attached to the main mirror only when they are needed.

Another helpful arrangement consists of a stationary center mirror and two hinged mirrors, one on each side, that can be swung to adjust the viewing angle. These three-way mirrors are sold as a unit, and some medicine cabinets also have them. You could even have one custom-made to fit a particular wall area or a particular corner.

Full-length mirrors are helpful too, although they are usually located in the dressing area, rather than in the bathing or grooming area. If the bathroom includes a special exercise space, there should be one or two full-length mirrors in it.

### Design Considerations
Mirrors can be used to expand the apparent space in a small bathroom or in a bathroom that is long and narrow. If one whole wall is covered with mirror, at least from the height of the counter to the ceiling, it makes the room appear twice as large. It also makes everything appear double, which could be distracting. Mirrors on adjacent walls that intersect at a corner create a fascinating effect and also tend to double the apparent size of the room. Mirrors on opposite walls create the familiar barbershop or beauty salon tunnel-to-infinity effect. This can be fun for your guests, but it might be disconcerting on a daily basis.

If you want to use mirrors to expand the space without overdoing it, the safest approach is to use one or two fairly large ones, 5 feet wide, say, by 3½ feet tall rather than floor-to-ceiling or wall-to-wall mirrors. If you use one large mirror, place it on one of the walls that form a right angle to the entry.

To plan the size of a mirror, line up the top, bottom, and sides with other features of the room—the top of a back splash, a windowsill, a corner where two walls intersect, the top of a door or a window, or a storage unit. This will give a preliminary mirror size for planning purposes. To arrive at the exact size, have the installer take on-site measurements before cutting.

### Decorative Details
There are several ways to dress up a mirror to give it drama and flair. One is to add some curves; possibilities include a round mirror, a semicircular mirror, or a triptych with the center mirror curved at the top. Another is to give it a decorative edge treatment, perhaps a beveled effect or a striking frame of wood or chrome. Edge treatments work best when there is empty wall space all around the mirror. This prevents visual conflicts with other corners or edges. Etched designs offer another way to glamorize a mirror; floral patterns are suited to a turn-of-the-century decor and abstract borders suggest the art deco period. Smoked glass can be used successfully if it is restricted to dark, sensuous designs.

Consider, too, whether you want any mounting hardware to show. Mirrors can be held with mounting clips at the top and bottom; or by adhesive on the back of the mirror, aided by a thin but visible support channel along the bottom edge. Finally, determine whether holes will have to be cut in the mirror to accommodate lights or electrical outlets.

*Opposite: A mirrored wall enlarges the perceived space within a room. Use mirrors in a bathroom both for their aesthetic qualities and for their functional value.*

# PLANNING UTILITIES

T he need to plan ahead for utilities cannot be over-emphasized. Well-placed lighting, convenient electrical outlets, good heating, and proper venting will contribute as much to the success of your project as any fixture, fitting, or finish that you choose.

In some ways—certainly from a practical standpoint—these are the most important choices that you will make. Remember that you can design a lovely room, but if no one can see it because the lighting is bad, or if it is inconvenient to use because you didn't install enough outlets, all your work will be for naught.

## Lighting

For safety and well-being, good lighting is essential; but lighting is also a dynamic design element that can transform an ordinary bathroom into an extraordinary showcase. Conversely, without proper lighting the most stylish bathroom with the most lavish fixtures and amenities will be flat and uninteresting.

*A small garden just outside this master bath gives bathers privacy and a lovely view. The lattice fence encloses just a few feet of the backyard—enough for a few plants and a small fountain. Always look beyond the walls of the bathroom as you refine your design in order to incorporate views and available light into the room.*

## Natural Light

Look first for ways to bring as much natural daylight into the bathroom as possible. Look beyond the walls to see whether there are unsuspected vistas that an added window could exploit. If there is already a window, you may want to enlarge it. However, light from only one source creates glare and high contrasts, so try to plan another window on a different wall or use a skylight to balance the light from the first window. Then consider enlarging the original window to make it a more dramatic focal point, to capture a view, or simply to

bring in more light. Converting a window to a French door or a miniature greenhouse is another excellent way to add design appeal and gain practical side benefits. A corner window constitutes a double light source and provides a stunning setting for a bathtub.

The need for privacy may make ordinary windows unacceptable. The traditional solution is to use diffused glass. An alternative is to place the windows high enough so that you can use clear glass and still preserve privacy. For a view of the sky, clear glass is recommended. Unlike diffused

glass, it does not create a claustrophobic feeling. Another stylish alternative is to replace the window with glass block. A third option is a skylight, which admits five times as much light as a window of the same size. Because most bathrooms are small, even a skylight 2 feet square will have a dramatic impact.

Some windows receive intense sunlight during certain times of the day and during certain seasons. Morning sun and winter sun are usually welcome, but you may need to provide shades to soften it. A west-facing window that is exposed to the afternoon sun and a clear skylight should be shaded from the outside during the summer months.

If the window is in a bathtub or shower enclosure, use clear glass doors or a clear plastic shower curtain to let as much light as possible into the bathroom. When planning windows around tubs and showers, keep safety in mind. Local codes specify how close you can carry standard window glass to the floor or to the rim of the tub. Beyond that point you must use tempered glass, safety plate, or other approved glazing.

## Artificial Lighting

The days of a single light fixture dangling from the center of the ceiling are long gone. In today's bathroom a variety of light sources and independent controls are used to create both ideal illumination and an ideal ambience. Artificial lighting should be designed to flatter people and objects, to enhance the positive features of the room, and to create interesting visual effects.

An effective lighting system provides overall illumination for the entire bathroom and concentrated illumination for specific tasks. Start by identifying the areas where light should be concentrated. Usually there is enough spillover from these task lights to provide general lighting as well.

One area that requires special lighting is the vanity. A person standing or sitting in front of the mirror should be bathed in soft, shadowless light. A single light source on the wall above the mirror or on the ceiling will throw harsh shadows. The ideal arrangement is to have lights on both sides of the mirror and a light above it. The former could be vertical bar lights (sometimes called theater lights or Hollywood lights), vertical fluorescent tubes, or vertical incandescent tubes. The illumination on each side should total approximately 75 to 120 watts for incandescent lights and 20 watts for fluorescent tubes. The lights should extend from a point approximately 6 to 12 inches above the countertop to a point approximately 6 to 6½ feet above the floor. The overhead light could be a fixture in the same style as the side lights, mounted horizontally on the wall above the mirror, or it could consist of two or three recessed ceiling fixtures shining straight down on the vanity top. Light bouncing off the mirror and other surfaces helps to eliminate any shadows. The overhead lights should total 100 to 120 watts if they are incandescent and 32 to 54 watts if they are fluorescent.

Another important area to illuminate is the bathtub. One or two recessed ceiling fixtures over the tub are usually sufficient. They should total 60 to 75 watts each. However, electrical codes specify that any electrical device around a bathtub or whirlpool must be at least 7½ feet above the flood rim of the tub or at least 5 feet away from the tub horizontally. An exception is made for recessed or surface-mounted ceiling fixtures that have a glass or plastic lens and no metal rim. Check with the local building inspection department for other regulations pertaining to bathroom lighting.

Any steps leading up to the tub should also be illuminated, either with a recessed ceiling fixture or with low-voltage strip lights mounted under the overhang of each step.

Don't forget to illuminate the shower. Here special ceiling fixtures for wet locations can be installed directly overhead. For incandescent fixtures a total of 60 watts is recommended. The toilet compartment may also require direct lighting to make it easy to read if there is insufficient ambient light. Incandescent fixtures should total 60 to 75 watts; fluorescent fixtures just 30 to 40 watts.

Besides illuminating certain areas for specific tasks, a good lighting system provides enough ambient light to eliminate shadows and stark contrasts and to illuminate the floor for purposes of safety. Mood lighting is important, too. Dimmers and separate switching can be used to create various lighting effects, and small spotlights on interesting focal points, such as a gleaming faucet or a potted plant, add drama to any bathroom.

The type of light you use will affect mood and perception. Incandescent light is soft and flattering to the complexion. Fluorescent light is harsh and cold if the tubes are designated as cool white. Warm-white and full-spectrum tubes are better for bathroom use.

Finally, different types of bathrooms require different types of lighting. A powder room can be fairly dark; it lends itself to dramatic mood lighting. A bathroom where grooming and other specific tasks are performed must be well lighted.

Consider too the users' special needs. A bathroom for older adults, who are sensitive to glare and require higher light intensities than younger adults, must have excellent illumination. The easiest solution is to use a color scheme with light, reflective colors and to increase the wattage capacity of the fixtures.

Because safety, health, energy, and convenience are all important factors in good lighting, and because light is also a major element in design, you may want to seek professional advice. A few hours of consultation will go a long way toward creating a well-lighted and dramatic bathroom.

## Heating

It would not be surprising if you ranked heating high on your priority list. A bathroom requires more heat than most other rooms. A comfortable temperature for most rooms of the home is around 70° F, but a bathroom should be at least 86° F to be comfortable. It is difficult and uneconomical to maintain air temperatures this high, so other heating strategies must be used.

### Room Heater

In planning a heating system, it is helpful to understand how the body perceives heat. Heat is constantly moving from warm objects or bodies to cooler objects or bodies. It can be transferred by conduction, convection or radiation. Conduction is the direct transfer of heat through a solid medium (for example, by touching a hot stove), and convection is transfer of heat through the air (for example, by means of a forced-air heating system). Radiation is the direct transfer of heat across space. If you stand in direct sunshine, you feel heat from the sun; as soon as you move into shade, you no longer feel heat. Conversely, the body radiates heat directly toward the cooler objects that surround it. This is especially true of the unclothed portions of the body. It is this transfer of heat through radiation that affects your body comfort the most. If the air temperature is 60° F, but you are surrounded by objects and surfaces that average 90° F, your body will not radiate heat toward those surfaces very rapidly, and you will feel warm. If the air temperature is 70° F and you are surrounded by objects that average 50° F, you will feel chilly as your body radiates heat out toward the cool surfaces.

A radiant heating system is ideal for a bathroom because it warms the surfaces in the room first and the air only indirectly. An electric wall heater, a baseboard heater, or radiant-heat lamps can be run at high intensity for a short time to create a radiant-heat source that directly warms the body. The alternative—heating the air—would take much longer.

If it is not possible to install a radiant-heating system in the bathroom, the options are to increase the output of the forced-air system by enlarging the duct or adding a new register, or to expand the hot-water system by adding a new radiator.

If your budget is limited and your bathroom heating needs amount to only an occasional cold morning or evening, you can simply plan to employ a portable heater. If a portable heater will fill your needs, all you have to consider is a safe electrical outlet for its use and storage for the heater when it is not needed.

You may want to consult with a specialist to determine the best type of heating system for your bathroom. If you already have a system that works well, simply keep it intact, or move a register or two if necessary.

*Keeping a bathroom well heated and well ventilated is one goal of every good design. A strip model heater provides plenty of warmth for this elegant master bathroom. Such a heater can be installed without cutting into the wall.*

## Water Heater

Make sure that you will have enough hot water. This is especially important if you are adding a bathroom. It may take a long time for the hot water to reach the bathroom if the water heater is in another part of the house. To solve this problem, insulate the hot-water pipes, run a continuous loop of hot-water piping (through which the hot water constantly circulates), or install a second water heater closer to the bathroom. Electric tank heaters can be installed almost anywhere because they require no flue and the 240-volt electrical line is much easier to run than the pipeline for a gas model. Gas and electric tankless water heaters heat the water as it runs through the unit. These heaters are small enough to fit inside a vanity or a small cabinet, and they will heat any amount of water.

Finally, you can buy towel warmers that are plumbed directly to the hot-water lines. These store instant hot water for the shower or tub and heat your towels while you bathe.

## Electrical Outlets

Provide at least one duplex receptacle outlet above the countertop and near the mirror to accommodate hair dryers, razors, and other electrical equipment. You may want to provide an outlet inside one of the cabinets so that the appliances that are stored there will always be plugged in. You should have an additional outlet at floor level for vacuum cleaners, waxers, and so forth.

You may also want to provide outlets for an exhaust fan, a clock, a radio, a TV, a towel warmer, and a 240-volt heater. Note that all bathroom outlets must be protected with GFCI devices.

If whirlpool equipment is in your plans, a special air switch or similar device is recommended. Spa, sauna, and whirlpool manufacturer's brochures list the specific electrical requirements for their equipment.

## Ventilation

A bathroom must have adequate ventilation to prevent the buildup of excessive moisture, mildew, and unpleasant odors. A window that can be opened and shut fulfills most code requirements for bathroom ventilation, but an exhaust fan that is ducted to the outside, not just to the attic, is practically a necessity. It can be installed in the ceiling, and it should have a switch that is separate from the light switch. Some fans are incorporated into a light fixture and have separate switches for the fan and the light. Try to locate the fan at the highest point of the ceiling if it is pitched, or in a skylight well if there is one. Otherwise place it near the shower or tub to intercept vapors as close to the source as possible. Fans are rated by the volume of air they move in one minute, measured as cubic feet per minute (CFM). The minimum size for most bathrooms is 50 CFM, but larger units are available. Consult the manufacturer's recommendations to determine the appropriate size for your room. Fans are also rated for sound. A sound level of 4 sones or less is desirable. Roof-mounted fans tend to be quieter than ceiling-mounted fans.

Although a window also provides ventilation and lets in fresh air, it may not exhaust steam and vapor efficiently if it faces into the prevailing breezes. The best method for removing steam and vapor without a fan is to install a working skylight. Motorized units open and close automatically. Manual units are cranked open by means of a long handle.

In cold climates, where an open window is usually undesirable, the only way to bring fresh air into the bathroom may be with an air-to-air heat exchanger. This device draws stale air out of the house, draws in fresh air, and uses the heat from the former to warm the latter. In a cold climate, fit the exhaust fan with a damper to prevent the back flow of cold air when the fan is not in use.

## Sound Control

Several design and construction techniques can be used to prevent bathroom noises from wafting into other parts of the home. The most effective method is to soundproof the walls. This can be done in a variety of ways. If you are gutting the bathroom and exposing the wall framing, the best soundproofing technique is to build a false wall inside the original wall, staggering the studs so that you can weave blanket insulation between them. A simpler but less effective technique is to attach sound insulation board or metal insulating channels to the studs before you apply the wallboard. The least effective technique is to install standard insulation in the stud cavities. With this method the sound will still carry through the studs themselves.

A careful layout also helps to control sound. Locate closets or built-in cabinet units where they will buffer noises from the bathroom, and do not place the bathroom door directly opposite the door to another room.

Sound can be controlled with careful construction as well. Look for spaces where noise may travel through walls, such as cracks along the floor or around electrical outlet boxes, and seal these spaces with caulk or insulation. Strap water pipes securely and wrap drainpipes in insulation to dampen noise. Insulate around the bathtub, both to control noise and to help retain heat. If sound travels through the heating ducts, you can line the first few feet of duct with special fiberglass insulating boards to absorb the sound before it travels very far.

# PLANNING FINISH MATERIALS

The floor, walls, ceiling, and window treatments are major visual features of a bathroom, but they do not necessarily require dramatic or exotic finishes.

In most cases they serve as a background for the various fixtures and details, complementing them and setting them off. In some cases the floor, walls, ceiling, or windows are dramatic design accents in their own right. Practical considerations, such as moisture resistance and ease of maintenance, will also influence your choice of finish materials.

## Floor Coverings

A bathroom floor should be safe, comfortable, water-resistant, beautiful, and easy to maintain. Because users will often be barefoot, avoid any flooring material that is likely to be slippery under wet feet, such as ceramic tile with a slick glaze or highly polished marble or granite. Many tile and stone products that appear slippery are surprisingly skid-resistant, so consult with a knowledgeable dealer before you eliminate all tile or stone flooring. Another safety consideration is hardness. Choose a resilient material if some users, such as older adults, are prone to disabling falls.

For maximum comfort the floor should not feel rough or have any sharp edges. Neither should it feel cold. Thermal comfort is a matter of individual tolerance, but if you are especially sensitive to chills you may want to avoid dense materials that conduct heat rapidly and will draw it

away from the body upon contact. Of course, a floor with radiant heating will have just the opposite effect: The denser the flooring, the more readily it will conduct heat upward to the body or into the room. Comfort is also affected by the hardness and smoothness of the material. Carpet is the softest floor covering; it always feels good under bare feet. Hard materials can also feel good if they are smooth, but if they are rough or irregular, they can feel uncomfortable. Resilient materials, such as vinyl or rubber goods, are cushioned to enhance comfort.

Bathroom floors are prone to water damage. The flooring itself should be impervious to moisture, and it should also prevent moisture from reaching the subfloor. Do not rely on the flooring alone to prevent water damage. Adequate heating, ventilation, and shower and tub enclosures are all just as important.

All floor coverings must be cleaned regularly, and some require periodic maintenance. Carpet should be washed frequently to control must and mildew. Marble must be sealed periodically to protect it from stains. Tile grout must be sealed to control both stains and mildew. Resilient (especially no-wax) flooring is very easy to maintain, but it may wear out sooner than other materials. Wood floors are sealed with hard finishes that should be renewed every few years to ensure protection.

Cleaning and maintenance will vary with use. If youngsters or pets will be tracking dirt and grit into the bathroom, consider a highly durable material that resists scratching, such as ceramic tile, or a material that disguises wear, such as heavy-duty resilient sheet flooring with a random pattern.

No single floor covering is ideal for all bathrooms. Each one has certain advantages and disadvantages, which you must weigh when you make your final choice.

## Design Considerations

The floor anchors the design. It ties all the elements of the design together, and it helps to highlight the dominant features of the room. In some cases a bold or unusual floor can be a dominant feature in itself, but in most bathrooms the floor plays a background role.

Because most bathrooms are small, bathroom floors lend themselves to strategies for making a small space appear larger. The most important consideration here is color. Light, neutral colors make a space feel larger, and using the same color for both the floor and the walls helps to expand the space even more. If the flooring has a pattern, it should be simple and uniformly textured. A bold pattern tends to overwhelm a small space. If you use tile, choose grout of the same or a similar color to make the floor appear larger; a contrasting color emphasizes the grid pattern and may make the floor—and the entire room—look small.

Dark colors can look warm and rich, and in some small bathrooms they may be appropriate for creating a cozy feeling of intimacy. However, be aware that they tend to show water spots, spills, and stains more readily than light colors.

The relatively small size of a bathroom floor makes it possible to use more expensive materials than you might otherwise consider. You might also think about combining materials; for instance, if the floor is a simple, neutral-colored tile or vinyl, try choosing a richly detailed rug for an accent.

**Opposite:** *Ceramic tile has been used in baths for centuries. Its durability and beauty are as appropriate to a modern bathroom as they were to the palaces of Alexander the Great. Both ceramic tile and glass block can be installed by any handy homeowner. Doing your own installation may save you enough money to allow you to splurge on materials.*

## Practical Considerations

Some materials may raise the level of the finish floor above that of the floor in the adjacent rooms. Most flooring materials are quite thin, and the difference in floor heights can usually be bridged with a threshold or a transition piece in the doorway. Be sure to take into consideration the thickness of the underlayment when you determine the height of the new floor. Floor tiles set in a mortar bed can be as much as 1½ inches thick. Brick or masonry units are thick too. If you want a smooth, continuous floor between rooms when you use these materials, you may have to drop the level of the subfloor.

Make sure that the floor structure is strong enough to support such heavy materials as masonry or stone or a tile floor set in a mortar bed. Even if the floor unit itself is structurally sound, any deflection or movement could cause cracking in the finish floor. (See page 103.)

## Materials

Ceramic tile is a popular floor covering for bathrooms. It is water-resistant, durable, and easy to clean, and it comes in a wide choice of colors and styles. It is also very hard, which means that it conducts heat rapidly, and reflects sounds easily, and that objects dropped on it will break. Floor tiles are harder than wall tiles, and many of them have nonskid surfaces suitable for bathroom use. Sizes range from ½-inch mosaics to 12-inch squares, but the most common sizes are 4-inch, 8-inch, and 12-inch squares. Unglazed tiles must be

sealed after they are installed to make them moisture resistant. The design possibilities for tile are almost limitless. You can mix colors and sizes, trim the floor with an attractive border, or include an occasional decorative tile for an accent. If you are using a different size of tile for the walls, lay the floor tiles diagonally so that the mismatched grout lines will not be distracting.

Dimensioned-stone tiles are cut from granite, slate, marble, or other natural stone. They resemble ceramic tile but possess the random patterns and subtle variations of a natural

material. Slate tends to be dark gray or green. Marble ranges from pure white and stark black to rich shades of salmon, rose, or green. Granite is typically a mottled black and white, but it can have a rose or green tint. Polished finishes can be very slippery when wet; dull or matte finishes are more suitable for bathroom floors. Marble, which is porous, stains very easily and must be sealed. Typically, dimensioned-stone tiles come in 12-inch squares.

Both ceramic and dimensioned-stone tiles that are installed using a thinset method in a wet area should

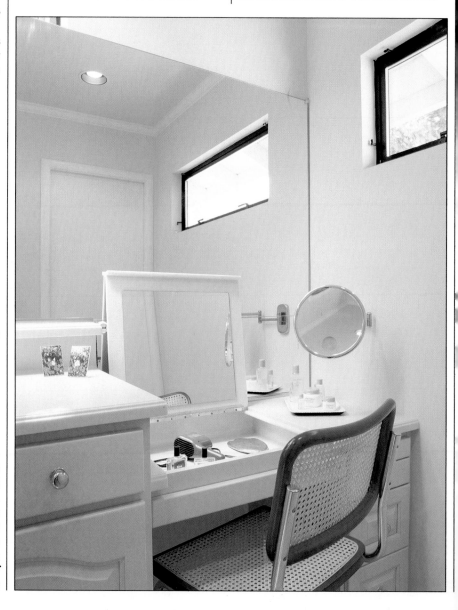

*A solid surface material lift-top vanity provides storage for frequently used items and makes it easy to clean up. Adjust the height of the vanity to accommodate uses that require either standing or sitting, and also to accommodate the height of the user.*

be laid over special tile-backing units. This makes installation easier, and it extends the life of the tile.

Resilient sheet materials, such as vinyl and linoleum, are very suitable for bathrooms. They are inexpensive, skid-resistant, water-resistant, and easy to maintain. They have a cushioned backing, come in a wide array of patterns and colors, and can be installed in most bathrooms with few, if any, seams. They are sold by the roll in 6-foot, 12-foot, and occasionally 9-foot widths. The best materials also have a wear layer—a clear layer of vinyl or urethane laid down over the pattern. Resilient materials can be scratched. For a high-traffic bathroom, choose a pattern that will not show scratches easily.

Resilient tiles are made of vinyl, rubber, or cork. They are usually the least expensive choice in flooring and the easiest to install, but they resist moisture poorly because of the many seams.

Carpet is the softest, most luxurious of the floor coverings. The unbroken expanse of color over a wide area also creates a feeling of serenity and simplicity. A bathroom carpet should have a synthetic backing to render it impervious to moisture. The pad should also be made of synthetic foam material, such as a rebond padding, to keep moisture from soaking through to the subfloor. A bathroom carpet should be cleaned regularly. For areas that are likely to be wet, cover the carpet with a bath mat or replace it with a water-resistant material, such as tile.

Wood floors can be used in bathrooms if they are sealed with several coats of polyurethane or a similar durable finish. Wood flooring that is finished and sealed after installation is preferable to prefinished products. Even properly sealed wooden floors are vulnerable to moisture over time. They are best used in powder rooms or in the drier parts of a bathroom. Square-edged seams withstand moisture much better than tongue-and-groove seams.

## Walls

The largest surface area of a bathroom is the walls, although windows, doorways, storage units, shower stalls, vanities, and fixtures will reduce this area considerably. Finish materials should be chosen for their good looks, moisture resistance, and ease of maintenance. The area around the tub or shower is especially important.

It is subject to direct water contact and should be finished with materials that are completely waterproof. The backing behind the finish materials is equally important; for most shower and tub installations it consists either of a mortar bed or of tile-backing units. Special moisture resistant wallboard is sometimes used in showers and tub surrounds, but it has largely been replaced by these tile-backing units. The rest of the walls can be covered with standard wallboard.

In most cases the easiest and most effective treatment for walls is to paint them a light, neutral color to emphasize the other features of the bathroom. Wallcoverings with small, subtle patterns are also very effective. The variations of color, texture, and motif add richness and warmth. Bold or busy wallcoverings can overwhelm a bathroom, but they can sometimes be used effectively to create design interest. However, when the walls are bold and striking, the fixtures and other features of the room should be plain and neutral colored so that they tend to recede into the background. Otherwise they will conflict with the wallcoverings or neutralize their impact.

### Paint

The least expensive wall treatment for bathrooms is paint. It comes in an unlimited range of colors, and it is easy to apply. Because bathrooms are damp, you should use a high-quality

alkyd or latex enamel over a recommended primer. Paint alone is not suitable for shower or tub enclosures that are exposed to direct spray.

Although paint is relatively inexpensive, it can look elegant when the color is well chosen. The most difficult color to work with is white. Pure white has blue in it and tends to look cold in a bathroom. Off-whites range from gray tones, which can look almost dirty next to gleaming white bathroom fixtures, to warmer tones with red or yellow in them. Off-whites with red and orange pigments will harmonize with oak or other wood trim. Off-whites with yellow pigments may work best with floral accents. Find a paint that matches the color of the dominant fixtures and experiment by mixing small amounts of it into a white base until you get a satisfactory off-white. Other colors can be custom mixed by a paint dealer.

Special techniques add excitement to any paint job. Sponging creates subtle variations in color and pattern that lend a fresh, dappled appearance to walls. It also creates an illusion of depth, which is very effective in small spaces. Faux marble, or veining, adds richness and elegance. Stenciling is an old American ornamental technique that has been revived in recent years. It can be used to create borders of vines, flowers, or other quaint figures to add a note of nostalgia or country freshness to the bathroom. A difficult technique—one that requires considerable skill—is to paint a mural or an architectural artifact in the trompe l'oeil tradition. The effect can be stunning. There are professional painters who specialize in this technique, transforming a blank wall into a window overlooking the pastoral countryside or a romantic courtyard.

Sometimes paint can be applied to a smooth wall to create a particular texture. Spray painting produces a perfectly flat, featureless surface for a sleek look. Lacquer finishes are an extreme example of this technique. A roller can be used to create orange peel or stippled textures, depending on how thick the paint is. These finishes have a uniformly bumpy appearance and require perfectly smooth walls. Other textures are produced by applying plaster or gypsum materials to the wallboard before it is painted. Skip-trowel or knockdown textures produce a pattern of flattened mesas all over the wall. Thick plaster finishes have a lumpy, handmade quality. Most of these texturing techniques produce an informal, casual effect.

## Wall Coverings

Vinyl and similar plastic wallcoverings can be effective in bathrooms. Ordinary wallpaper and foil papers can also be used, but not where they will be subjected to direct water or heavy condensation. None of these papers is suitable for shower or tub surrounds. Wallcoverings add pattern to the bathroom walls and can be used to carry out a theme. For a large space choose a pattern with small, widely separated motifs to keep the wallcovering from overwhelming the room. If you like a particularly bold or busy pattern, consider using it on only one wall.

## Tile

The classic wall finish for bathrooms is ceramic tile, especially for tub and shower enclosures and in the areas around other plumbing fixtures. Tile has a smooth, durable surface that resists moisture, is easy to clean, and looks new for years and years. Wall tiles, which are usually thinner and more brittle than floor tiles, come in a vast array of colors and patterns that can be combined to produce a wide variety of effects. For a crisp, clean look, use tiles that are uniformly regular. For a more informal look, use tiles that show variations in texture or color. Some tiles are manufactured with irregular surfaces that make them look handmade. You can even have tiles made to order with your own design.

Dimensioned-stone tiles (see page 48) can be used on vertical surfaces, provided they are not too thick. Check with the dealer or the installer during the planning stage to make certain that the tiles you choose are thin enough to stay on the walls.

There are no set rules for using tile. You can use it for special areas, such as back splashes or tub enclosures; as a wainscoting; or as a continuous finish all the way up the wall to the ceiling—and even across it. Contrasting colors or variations in the layout can be used to create borders and other designs that tie different elements of the room together. Decorative tiles can liven up a large expanse of wall.

## Slab Materials

Large slabs of natural marble and granite or of cultured marble or solid surface materials can create luxurious-looking walls with few seams. These walls resist moisture and are easy to clean, although marble will stain if it is not sealed properly. Many slab materials are expensive. They should be installed professionally. They are used most commonly in showers and tub surrounds, but they can look very dramatic on other wall surfaces as well. Slabs of natural stone are extremely heavy, so if you plan to use it extensively have an architect, structural engineer, or experienced contractor check the structure of the bathroom walls and floor to determine whether they should be reinforced.

## Laminates

High-pressure plastic laminates are usually associated with cabinets and countertops, but they can also be used to cover walls. The intense colors and durable surface allow you to create exciting effects. Laminates come in 4-foot widths; this is often wide enough to make possible a seamless installation.

## Ceiling

As you concentrate on the floor plan and the elevations, it is very easy to overlook the ceiling, but the ceiling is an important element in the design. Any variation from a standard 8-foot flat ceiling adds interest and drama to a room. However, variations must be used carefully in a bathroom. A high ceiling makes most rooms feel formal, and this may not be appropriate for a bathroom, which should feel intimate and relaxed. A high ceiling may also overwhelm a small bathroom. If the ceiling is too high, you can create the illusion of a lower ceiling by adding a painted or tiled border strip around the wall at the 8-foot level. You can even install a false ceiling. A ceiling of several different heights creates a feeling of movement and animation, which may not be appropriate for a space that should feel relaxed. A skylight or other interruption acts as a focal point. Beams and soffits can be used to alter the apparent shape of a room. A beam that runs across the narrow dimension of a long room makes it feel more square, for example. A soffit can be used to define the tub area or the vanity area. It also creates a space in which to conceal recessed light fixtures for focused lighting.

The color of a ceiling has a strong effect on the apparent space. A light ceiling feels higher, a dark ceiling feels lower. A ceiling that is the same hue as the walls but slightly lighter will almost disappear. A patterned ceiling will draw the eye upward; however, if the pattern is busy or bold, the ceiling will feel even closer.

A bathroom ceiling can be finished with any material that can be used on the walls, except heavy slabs. Tile on ceilings is usually restricted to tub or shower enclosures. A full tile ceiling can feel institutional. Ceilings of cedar, redwood, or similar durable wood can work very well in a bathroom, giving it a natural or rustic feeling. Paint and wallcoverings are the most popular ceiling finishes, and the least expensive.

## Window Treatments

Well-chosen windows add drama to any room. They offer views, bring in daylight, and help to make a small space look bigger. To be effective, the window and the window treatment must harmonize with the overall design to create a sense of purpose and place. The size and location of the windows; the type, style, and shape of the frame and glass; and the window coverings should all be planned with careful consideration.

Start by choosing the type of glass. If the view is pleasant and privacy is not an issue, use clear glass. Otherwise use diffused glass, which has a frosted, translucent quality. One-way, or mirrored, glass is another option. It presents a reflective surface to the outside but lets you see out from the inside. If the window is exposed to intense sunlight during hot weather, consider tinted heat-reflecting glass.

Dress up an ordinary window with stained glass. The simplest way to do this is to hang a stained glass panel in front of the bathroom window. For a more individualized look you can remove the window sash and have the original pane replaced with a custom-made stained glass design. A less costly option is a stained glass overlay, which is created by applying transparent, glasslike materials to the original windowpane. Many local glass shops offer this service. You could even have the design repeated on the shower doors or the mirrors.

Other window treatments include shutters, blinds, and curtains. Wood shutters should be painted with a good enamel paint or, if they are stained, sealed with polyurethane to protect them against moisture damage. The hardware should also be solid brass rather than steel plated with brass or some other finish. Otherwise it can easily rust in a humid bathroom. If the hardware is steel (you can find out by checking it with a magnet), coat it with a clear plastic sealer to prolong the untarnished look. Blinds add a touch of contemporary elegance to a bathroom. Some double-glazed windows come with microblinds already installed between the panes. When you buy window blinds for a bathroom, choose high-quality products with a plastic coating over the metal slats. Otherwise the metal slats can rust.

Curtains add a note of romance, and they soften hard bathroom surfaces. Chintzes, lace, and light-colored patterns fit in with many of today's airy bathroom designs. Most fabrics can withstand the humidity in a bathroom as long as the room is heated and ventilated properly, but a knowledgeable fabric dealer can help you to make the best selection for your particular bathroom.

*Adding an outside access door gave this bathroom a dual purpose. The room is the master bath and now also serves patio guests, who can reach it without having to go through the house.*

# PLANNING ACCESSORIES

**M**any beautiful and luxurious bathrooms were completed before anyone realized that they contained no place to hang up a towel. Some people think of towel bars and similar accessories as afterthoughts that can be dealt with later, but on a day-to-day basis they are among the most important features of a bathroom.

A hamper or a laundry chute is a handy feature in any bathroom. A large open basket fits well into many design schemes. There may be enough space for a small hamper inside a storage cabinet or a vanity. Just be sure that any closed space has enough ventilation to prevent mildew and odors from forming.

Other accessories to consider are cabinet hardware, a toilet paper holder, a soap dish, magazine and book racks, bathtub toy storage for a family bathroom, holders for toothbrushes and a tumbler, caddies for shower accessories, and bathrobe hooks. Try to include all of these things in your floor plan and elevation sketches. If you assume that they can be added later, your sleek, crisp bathroom design may be overwhelmed by a clutter of small details.

In some cases, new accessories, new paint, and perhaps a new faucet or two may be all the rejuvenation that the bathroom needs. Whether or not the accessories are part of a larger plan, they must be coordinated with the overall design.

## Towel Bars

Would you rather display your towels prominently or tuck them away discreetly? In either case, plan the places where you will store them as carefully as any other part of the design. First look for available wall space on which to mount towel bars. Standard lengths are 18, 24, 30, 36, and 42 inches. A comfortable height is 36 to 48 inches above the floor, although higher bars are acceptable above a countertop. Towel rings are an option, especially for hand towels, where wall space is limited. Try out different locations on your elevation sketches. Be sure to include enough space for the towels to hang. Allow at least 18 inches of clear space below the bar for a hand towel, 12 inches for a guest towel, and 30 inches for a bath towel.

If there is not enough wall space on which to hang towels, or if you do not want to display them prominently, consider mounting the towel bars on the back of a door, the side of a vanity, or inside a well-ventilated closet. You might also want to hang towels inside the shower stall. If you prefer simply to toss large towels into a hamper after using them, provide at least a hook near the shower or bathtub on which to hang a fresh towel before you take a bath.

## Rugs

Whatever floor covering you decide on for your bathroom, you still must plan for some kind of rug to step on after a shower or bath. Consider the size of rug you'll need when determining your layout. Rugs made especially for bathroom use come in a wide variety of colors and sizes, often as part of matching towel sets. Other options include handmade rag rugs, oriental tapestry designs, or fluffy lambs wool throws. Specialty rugs can act as a wonderful focal piece of an unusual bathroom theme.

Be sure that the rug you choose is backed with a skid-proof surface or that you lay a skid-proof mat beneath the rug to prevent slips. If you do not want the rug on the floor all of the time, plan a convenient, well-ventilated storage place where it can be hung to dry between uses.

## Storage

If yours is like most households, storage ranks high on your bathroom priority list. Planning for storage involves more than merely looking for a place to hang a cabinet. First identify your storage needs. Decide exactly what you want in the bathroom, where it should go, and how much space it will require.

### Closets

High on most people's wish list is a full closet, with shelves for towels and other necessities and space to hang robes and clothing. If there is a bedroom closet on the backside of one of the bathroom walls, you may be able to partition off part of it and put a door in the bathroom wall. If there is space at the end of the bathtub or in a corner, you may be able to build a new closet. Wardrobe closets are usually 24 inches deep, but a shallower closet will hold shelves and a clothes hook or two, if a shallower closet is all that you have room for. Another option is to buy a prefabricated unit. Many modular furniture lines include closets. They are usually finished in white or neutral laminates that harmonize with many bathroom designs.

*Opposite: Warmed towels were once found only in the finest hotels. Today, towel warmers for private homes are available in several styles and in a range of finishes. Some towel warmers are electric; others are plumbed and serve as miniature water heaters while providing instant hot water for the bath or shower.*

### Cabinets

Several types of modular cabinets are designed specifically for use in bathrooms. They include wall units that fit above the toilet, hampers, base units that double as comfortable seats, and tall storage units.

Many standard kitchen cabinets can also be used in the bathroom. Base units are 24 inches deep, and wall units are 12 inches deep; widths range from 18 to 48 inches in 3-inch increments.

If space is tight, you can cut down a wall unit. A cabinet only 8 inches deep provides plenty of room for towels and most bathroom supplies. Bear in mind that wall units need not be confined to the upper wall. They can be installed from floor to ceiling to create a roomy, integrated storage system.

Custom cabinets can be built to size to fit any available space. They usually look less obtrusive than single modular units because they can be aligned with other features in the room and finished with the same materials. With custom-made cabinets you can consolidate all of the storage onto one wall, along with the vanity and a mirror, leaving the other three walls free.

Antique dressers, armoires, china cabinets, or collection cases are appropriate in many bathroom settings. They may fit into a period scheme or provide a nostalgic accent in a modern setting. They need not fit perfectly in the available space in order to look extremely handsome.

### Shelves

Some bathroom accessories are best stored on open shelves. A stack of freshly laundered towels can be very attractive, and many bathroom products are designed for open display. A set of shelves can be hung above the toilet or below a window. Single shelves can go almost anywhere and be any size, from a narrow glass unit above the washbasin to a continuous shelf across one whole wall. Unusual materials, such as granite or marble, make a small shelf go a long way. If the bathroom is too small to hang any shelves at the usual height, consider a shelf over the top of the door. It could even be extended to provide high storage for the full length of one or two walls, freeing up floor space and wall space.

Shelves can also be built into walls. A simple alcove finished in plaster would make a stunning display for rolled-up towels. Glass shelves set into a small tiled alcove would enhance the beauty of the tile as well as objects on display. A cluster of small alcoves and nooks might be an intriguing alternative to a single cabinet or shelf.

### Telephone

As bathrooms have become less like chemistry labs and more like living spaces, they have acquired many of the traditional comforts of home. One of the first conveniences to make its way from other rooms into the bathroom was the telephone, now practically standard in new or remodeled baths. Outlets near the toilet are routinely wired into new homes, and cordless models make it possible to talk on the telephone while you are in the bathtub.

*Dirty clothes hampers built into the vanity save space in a small family bathroom.*

## Entertainment System

If you enjoy having a radio in the bathroom, you might consider installing a stereo. Large luxury bathrooms often have a TV or a full entertainment center that includes a VCR, a stereo, and other electronic equipment. The wiring must be protected by a ground fault circuit interrupter (GFCI) to prevent the possibility of electric shock. Remote controls make electronic equipment even safer to use in the bathroom.

## Fireplace

Another way to transform an ordinary bathroom into a warm, cozy retreat is to install a fireplace. Zero-clearance models, with metal fireboxes and flue pipes, are relatively easy to install and can fit into a space only 30 inches wide by 24 inches deep. Special wood-burning stoves designed for boats can fit into even smaller spaces, as long as specified clearances from combustible surfaces are maintained. Consult with the local building inspection department before you install any wood-burning devices.

## Furniture

There is no reason why furniture meant for other rooms cannot be used in a bathroom if it serves a need and complements the overall design. A comfortable chair makes dressing and undressing, or simply relaxing, a pleasure. A valet will help keep clothes fresh if the bathroom is used as a dressing room. A desk and chair or a dressing table might also be appropriate.

*A lot of laundry is generated in a bathroom, so consider putting the laundry center right in the room. The closet runs the width of this bath, providing a large linen storage area behind the toilet. Bifold doors conceal the appliances when not in use.*

## Fitness Center

A large bathroom is a natural candidate for a fitness center. It might also be possible to use an adjacent outdoor area or family room for the activities and place the equipment and other amenities in the bathroom. In planning a fitness center, consider a whirlpool system, a sauna or steam room, a music system, a TV with VCR for playing exercise tapes, and plenty of ventilation.

An exercise area could have large mirrors; extensive lighting on dimmer controls; a padded bench or two; a ballet bar; and specialized equipment, such as a stationary cycle and a weight-lifting machine or a rowing machine. In order to see the benefits of your labors, remember to put a scale in the room.

## Art

The bathroom is an excellent place in which to display art. This is especially true of a powder room, which contains no shower or tub. Sculpture, ceramics, art glass, and other durable pieces can generally withstand the most extreme conditions and are ideal for bathrooms.

A properly ventilated bathroom, where the temperature is stable and moisture is controlled, may be appropriate for framed poster art, some oil paintings, photographs, and fabric works, but for watercolors or any valuable art, use extreme caution. Consult with a professional artist, art collector, or restorer before you display these pieces in a bathroom.

# BATHROOM PLANNING FOR THE PHYSICALLY CHALLENGED

Besides the normal safety precautions that are recommended for any bathroom, there are special features that you must consider in planning a bathroom for someone whose mobility, vision, or other faculties are impaired. You may want to consider these features in any case.

## Space Planning

For wheelchair users the entrance to the bathroom should be wide enough for easy passage. A pocket door is the easiest to maneuver from a wheelchair. A conventional door should swing outward, and there should be enough room on the outer side to maneuver the wheelchair while opening the door. There should be enough space inside the bathroom to turn the wheelchair around.

A bathroom for an ambulatory person who has limited mobility should have nonskid flooring and grab bars in the entry and next to the toilet, tub, and shower. A narrow floor plan is ideal because a bar can be installed at waist level all along one wall; such a bar is always within reach. Consult with a knowledgeable dealer or with the user's physician or physical therapist to determine the best type of

grab bar, and the best place to install it, for each fixture. Grab bars now come in a variety of decorator colors and styles that are less institutional looking than the traditional stainless steel variety. Avoid placing towel bars, which are not as firmly anchored, at the same level as grab bars—one could easily be mistaken for the other. One safe approach would be to use grab bars to hold towels, as well.

The toilet should be next to a sidewall so that grab bars can be mounted on both walls. There should be at least 48 inches of clear space on one side of the toilet for wheelchair access, although some users may prefer to park in front of the toilet. An extrahigh fixture (3 inches higher than a conventional toilet) is more convenient for many users. A wall-mounted model has no

obstruction near the floor and allows for easier maneuvering. There are many grab-bar arrangements for toilets; one of the best includes an overhead bar that a wheelchair user can hang onto while transferring from the wheelchair to the toilet.

The washbasin can be adapted for specific needs. For a wheelchair user there should be enough clearance under the basin to pull up close. This usually means raising the drainpipe and the water supply pipes and installing a shallow basin. Insulate the exposed water pipes and the drainpipe with foam materials to prevent accidental scalding or cold shocks. Make sure that there are no sharp, protruding objects under the basin. Some basins can be moved up and down on stationary guides to suit individual needs. The faucet handles should be easy to reach. Some

*A wall-mounted sink set lower than usual, a low-model toilet, and specially installed grab bars make daily functions easier for a child in a wheelchair. The room need not look sterile, however, as documented by this beautifully tiled bath.*

faucets have levers long enough to be operated by the wrists or forearms.

A shower is more convenient to use than a bathtub and can be adapted for special use. A shower with no curb is preferable. When you install it, slope the floor toward the drain and consider providing a second drain outside the shower area in case of backups. Include a shower seat, nonslip grab bars, a single-handle lever control, and a hand-held sprayer.

A bathtub can be difficult for a disabled person to get into, but a hydraulic lift or a continuous bench over the rim that extends from inside to outside the tub area can help. A nonskid bottom, grab bars with a nonslip surface, a hand-held sprayer, and conveniently located controls should be included with the bathtub.

## Minimum Clearances

Even if you are not designing a bathroom for a disabled person, consider your family's long-range needs.

For wheelchair use, the door should be at least 32 inches wide. The hallway area should provide at least 44 inches of clearance for turning into the doorway and pushing the door open easily. Within the bathroom there must be at least 60 inches of clearance in which to turn around.

The toilet should have 32 inches of clear space on one side and 48 inches in front. A shower stall should be 60 inches in diameter and have a bench or seat. Smaller stalls can be fitted with grab bars to make access possible.

## Planning for Safety

Help to prevent unfortunate home accidents with a safety-conscious design and careful use of the bathroom. Start with a floor plan that allows easy freedom of movement. Then choose a skid-resistant floor covering. Finally, use common sense. This checklist offers more specific suggestions.

☐ Provide lockable storage for all medications.

☐ Store cleaning agents and other dangerous materials out of reach of youngsters.

☐ Protect all electrical outlets with GFCI devices.

☐ Provide enough outlets to eliminate the need for extension cords.

☐ Place light switches at heights that are convenient for every member of the family.

☐ Do not store things that are used daily in places that are hard to reach.

☐ Avoid any one-step changes in the floor level.

☐ Be sure that all floor areas and task areas are well lighted.

☐ Get proper permits for all work done on the bathroom.

☐ Install electrical fixtures, appliances, and whirlpool equipment according to the manufacturer's instructions and the local codes.

☐ Install a door lock that can be opened from the outside with a nail or other common device.

☐ Plan the doorswing so that it does not open into a traffic corridor and, if possible, so that the door would not be blocked by someone who had fallen on the floor.

☐ Use temperature control faucets in the shower, tub, and washbasin.

☐ Provide a security lock on any window that is left partially open.

☐ Maintain privacy by blocking any view from a public area with fencing or some other screening device.

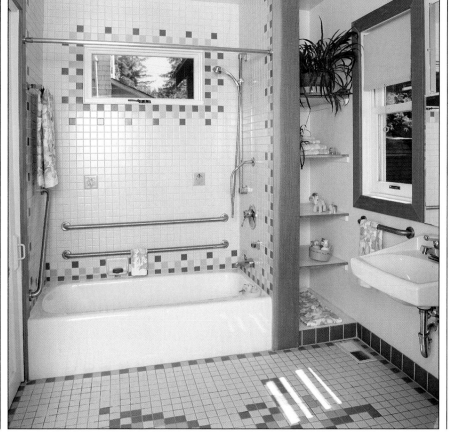

*A bathroom adapted for disabled access should include a tub that is lower than usual, an adjustable showerhead, and grab bars.*

# FINALIZING THE DESIGN

*I*t may take months to consider all of the design factors and to refine the bathroom plan, but there will come a time when you are ready to produce the final plan drawings and material specifications.

Finalizing your design includes drawing a detailed floor plan and elevations (see page 19), and preparing a list of all of the materials and fixtures that you will need to buy. You may need only a floor plan to obtain a permit for a simple remodeling project, but you will need the elevations and the specifications list as well if you intend to consult with a designer, to work up a detailed estimate, to solicit bids, to coordinate subcontractors, and to traffic ordered materials.

This hard work and careful planning of refining the design will pay off when you begin to plan the project and to do the actual construction. These next two phases are covered in the third and fourth chapters respectively.

If you enjoy designing and remodeling bathrooms, consider putting together a working scrapbook of your project. In a ring binder, place "before" photographs, your base and preliminary plans, your cost estimates, the final plan, and the materials specifications list. You might also include invoices. At the end of the project, add final photographs and perhaps your thoughts on the parts of the project that went well and how other parts could have gone more smoothly. Besides having a fun memento of the project, you'll also have a complete guide should you choose to perform another remodeling project in the future.

## Design Checklist

Consider the following suggestions to avoid the most common pitfalls of bathroom layout.
☐ Be aware of minimum clearance requirements for each fixture (see pages 22 and 57).
☐ Try to exceed the minimums whenever possible.
☐ Include doorswings and wall thicknesses in your drawings.
☐ Avoid placing a washbasin where it will be necessary to shut the access door to use it.
☐ If two people will share the bathroom, be sure that the fixtures can be used simultaneously. If the toilet and basin are at right angles to each other, provide enough space to use both at once. Avoid placing two fixtures directly opposite each other unless there is at least 48 inches between them.
☐ Try to maintain open sight lines to enhance the feeling of space. For instance, make sure the window view can be seen from the entry or from the toilet.
☐ Provide an unobstructed view from the bathtub, either out a window or towards a piece of art.
☐ Eliminate unpleasant views into the bathroom. For instance, avoid a direct view of the toilet when the bathroom door is open.
☐ Allow extra space for larger fixtures, such as an elongated toilet bowl or a large washbasin.
☐ Consider the space needed for general circulation and for engaging in various activities.
☐ Provide enough room for comfortably dressing and undressing and for toweling off after bathing.
☐ Provide open wall space for towel bars, clothes hooks, and art displays.
☐ Allow sufficient towel and paper product storage.
☐ Provide a safe storage cabinet for medicines and cleaning products.

## Material Specifications

Using your cost estimate lists and final floor plan as a starting point, make up a final materials list that includes all the information you need to order specific items for your new bathroom. Noting something as "white countertop" is no longer sufficient. Now you must know exactly the material, brand, and exact color of each item planned for your new room.

This list will also serve as a tracking system. Using this list you'll be able to plan deliveries and storage needs, to tell any workers when they can expect various materials, and to adjust other elements should a desired item become unavailable. Update this list regularly and keep it handy.

Some people will find this list more valuable in chart form, especially if it is to be used by several people, such as you, your designer, your contractor, and various subcontractors.

Be sure to indicate the date of all orders and changes. For each item, you'll find it helpful to have the following information.
☐ Item
☐ Manufacturer
☐ Name and model number
☐ Color including name and dye lot, if applicable
☐ Material
☐ Size or measurements
☐ Quantity
☐ Unit price
☐ Total price including tax and delivery charges
☐ Date ordered
☐ Place ordered
☐ Name of individual through whom you ordered
☐ Projected date of delivery
☐ Actual date of delivery
☐ Second choice
☐ Items affected by change
☐ Attach order receipts, if applicable

**Opposite:** *One tall person and one short person share this master bath. A two-tiered countertop gives each of them a convenient washbasin.*

# PROJECT PLANNING

**P**lanning for construction is critical if you want to transform your dreams into a beautiful new bathroom. You may be tempted to begin the actual remodeling as soon as you have completed the design, but a successful project depends on planning everything out in advance. Whether you will manage the project yourself or hire a general contractor to do it, construction should not begin until you have a firm estimate of costs, adequate financing, a realistic time line, a clear understanding of who will be doing what, a list of the materials required to complete the job, and the proper permits. To some extent any remodeling project is a journey into the unknown. Planning every aspect of the project as thoroughly as possible ahead of time is the best way to avoid surprises, setbacks, and disappointments. The more effort you put into these preliminary tasks, the more successful and enjoyable the job will be.

*Luxury spas are used as physical therapy pools in many homes; they are a welcome sight after a hard workout or long jog. This spa, located off the family room, holds up to six people. The windows next to it can be completely removed and the skylight opened, giving the space an indoor-outdoor feeling.*

# ESTIMATING COSTS

One of the most important—and most difficult—skills in construction is to estimate the cost of the project. For an accurate estimate you will need final plans and material specifications. You can make an estimate of costs using the principles outlined in this section or you can hire a contractor to give an estimate.

Do not rely on your own preliminary plans or on a designer's estimate of projected costs or on any contractor's price that is not a firm bid based on the final plans. Plans and specifications should include all proposed changes to the structure; the locations of all plumbing, electrical, heating, and ventilating devices; the type of flooring materials, finish wall and ceiling materials; trim details; window and door specifications; cabinet sizes; and the model and manufacturer of each plumbing and electrical fixture. These specifications will enable you and the contractor, subcontractors, suppliers, and consultants to account for every detail.

If the project involves remodeling an existing bathroom, allow for the unexpected as well. Quite often, what starts out as a simple rejuvenation project becomes more involved once you begin demolition. Some of the surprises you may find include more involved plumbing changes than originally planned, previously undiscovered water or insect damage, or a personal desire to make a few additional changes once the project begins.

## Contractors' Bids
If you are hiring a general contractor or several subcontractors, their bids will be the estimate. Be sure that you understand what is and is not included in each bid. For instance, who will be responsible for removing debris? For purchasing and installing fixtures? For painting? If your plans do not specify such details as type of tile, brand of sink faucet, or type of cabinet hardware, clarify whether the

## Sample Breakdown for Installing Standard Bathtub and Shower

| Task | Materials | Tools | Labor |
|------|-----------|-------|-------|
| Alter framing | 2x4s, 1x4s, nails | Hammer, saw, tape measure | ½ hour |
| Rough in drain | 1½" P-trap, pipe, fittings, glue | Pipe cutter, tape measure | ½ hour |
| Rough in supply pipes and valve | Faucet, ½" pipe and fittings, faucet, stubs | Pipe cutter or saw, pipe-joining materials, wrenches, tape measure | 1 hour |
| Install tub | Bathtub, shims | Dolly, runners | ½ hour |
| Hook up drain | Trip-lever unit, putty, Teflon tape | Wrenches, screwdrivers, hacksaw | 1 hour |
| Insulate tub | Blanket insulation | Knife | ¼ hour |
| Insulate wall | Insulation, plastic sheeting, staples | Knife, tape measure, stapler | ½ hour |
| Prepare for tile | Tile backing board, nails, tape, corner bead, joint compound, sealer | Knife, hammer, tape measure, joint knife | 1 hour |
| Paint (touch up) | Primer, finish coat, thinner | Brushes, roller, drop cloth | ½ hour |
| Install tile | Adhesive, tile, trim pieces, spacers | Buckets, tile cutter, tape measure, nippers, trowel | 3 hours |
| Grout tile | Grout, additive | Buckets, rubber float, sponges, cheesecloth | 2 hours |
| Install finish plumbing | Faucet flange and handles, spout, showerhead | Screwdrivers, wrenches | ¼ hour |
| Apply caulk | Silicon caulk | Caulking gun, rags | ½ hour |

bids include a certain allowance for these items. If the bids assume that cheap materials will be used, you will have to pay the difference if you want to use more expensive materials. Also try to identify places where problems may arise, or where you may decide to opt for additions that would require a change order. This too involves extra expense.

## Doing Your Own Estimate

If you are acting as your own general contractor, you will have to do the cost estimate yourself. There are several methods for estimating costs; these include using square footage multiples and comparing your project to similar projects of known cost. However, the only reliable way to estimate a job is to break it down into separate phases, itemize the materials and labor costs for each phase, total them up, and add a reasonable contingency factor to the total.

If you plan to hire subcontractors for some of the work, use their bids as estimates for those phases. For the rest of the project, use a work sheet similar to the one on the opposite page, basing it on your plans and on the construction information in the fourth chapter. To price materials, make a complete list and shop around at various suppliers.

The cost estimate should include a contingency factor, usually 5 to 10 percent, to cover cost overruns.

## Hidden Costs

Most of the costs of a building project are predictable; costs for remodeling less so. Although most items are in the plans that you spent a great deal of time deciding about, there are hidden costs as well. These costs are easy to overlook, and they can add up significantly over the course of a long project.
☐ Permit fees
☐ Employer expenses for hiring labor (payroll taxes, Workers' Compensation insurance)

☐ Tools, either to buy or to rent
☐ Sharpening or replacing blades
☐ Power cords and lights
☐ Safety equipment: goggles, gloves, dust masks, painter's masks, respirators, work boots, hard hats
☐ Vehicle mileage, wear and tear
☐ Increased use of telephone and utilities
☐ Debris box rental or dump fees
☐ Tarps or plastic sheeting to cover supplies or to protect surfaces.
☐ Replacing inadequate plumbing lines "while we're at it"
☐ Improving the electrical system "while we're at it"
☐ Replacing baseboards to go with new flooring
☐ Inability to recycle existing materials as originally planned
☐ Patching the roof or siding around new plumbing vents, duct outlets, windows, or skylights
☐ Enlarging a deck or porch to accommodate new exterior doors
☐ Delivery charges for materials
☐ Insulating exterior walls you hadn't intended to open up
☐ Cleanup
☐ New window coverings, accessories, plants

## Obtaining Financing

Unless you are able to pay for a new bathroom out of pocket, you will have to do some financial planning to determine your budget and arrange for financing. Most lenders require the following information, and it will also help you to set a realistic budget.

Before meeting with a lender, you will need to know the following.
1. Your total net worth
2. Anticipated new expenses (a baby, a car, college tuition)
3. Your expected cash flow during the design and construction phases (and afterwards, if you obtain a loan)
4. Your borrowing power

To figure your net worth, follow these steps.
1. Total your assets (cash, savings accounts, checking accounts, stocks, bonds, securities, surrender value of life insurance, market value of real estate, automobiles, furnishings, jewelry, pension funds).
2. Total your liabilities (real estate loans, accounts and contracts payable, installment loans).
3. Subtract total liabilities from total assets to find your net worth. These are assets that you can liquidate or pledge as security for a loan.

To figure your estimated net monthly cash flow, follow these steps.
1. Total your current monthly income (net wages, investment income, monthly value of health and other benefits).
2. Total your current monthly expenses (mortgages, auto loans, property taxes, insurance payments, installment and credit card payments, living expenses).
3. Subtract expenses from income to get current net monthly cash flow.
4. Project your net monthly cash flow for the next five years by adding any expected new income and subtracting any anticipated new expenses. Be sure to include new monthly expenses that will be incurred by the improvements to the bathroom, such as increased insurance premiums or property taxes.
5. Average your current and projected net monthly cash flow to obtain your estimated net monthly cash flow. This will give you a realistic idea of how much money will be available every month to pay back a new loan.

You should also consider the value of your home, both now and after you have remodeled the bathroom, to help you to arrive at a realistic budget. If you need help, consult with a local real estate agent or hire a professional appraiser.

Once you have determined your budget and have estimated the cost of the project, obtain the financing so that funds will be available when you begin construction.

# SCHEDULING THE PROJECT

A detailed time line helps you to negotiate contracts, schedule your own time, and estimate the date of completion. The first step in preparing a time line is to establish the sequence of construction. The actual sequence will vary from job to job, but the following example is typical of most bathroom projects that do not involve an addition or other major structural changes.

## Preconstruction

1. Complete design.
2. Obtain bids or work up an estimate.
3. Prepare a time line.
4. Arrange for financing.
5. Hire a contractor or subcontractors as needed.
6. Order any materials and fixtures that have long delivery times (cabinets, custom fixtures, windows, fireplace).
7. Obtain permits.
8. Make arrangements to use another bathroom, if necessary.
9. Arrange for the removal of debris and for the storage of materials.

## Demolition

10. Clear out all movable items.
11. Seal off the bathroom from the rest of the house.
12. Remove shelves and built-in storage units.
13. Remove washbasin, countertop, and vanity.
14. Remove trim and moldings.
15. Remove toilet and seal the drain opening.
16. Remove or repair floor covering if necessary.
17. Remove lights and electrical fixtures.
18. Remove wall and ceiling materials, such as tile, plaster, or plasterboard as needed.
19. Remove bathtub or shower pan.

## Preparing the Space

20. Remove or alter walls; shore up bearing walls.
21. Repair subfloor if necessary.
22. Complete rough framing for alterations, new walls, soffits, windows, and doors.
23. Install new windows, skylights, and exterior doors.
24. Install new heating and venting ducts if needed.
25. Alter or install rough plumbing.
26. Install new tub, shower, or shower pan.
27. Alter or install rough wiring.
28. Install fan.
29. Get preliminary inspections.
30. Install insulation and get it inspected if required.
31. Repair, replace, or install wallboard; apply finish.
32. Install door and window trim, except where it will be fitted around cabinets.
33. Paint ceiling, walls, and trim.
34. Install tile or similar wallcoverings.
35. Install flooring, including underlayment. Some types of flooring may be installed later in the project.
36. Install interior doors.

## Installing Finish Materials and Fixtures

37. Install cabinets, cabinet trim, and other storage units.
38. Install countertops and back splashes.
39. Install baseboards and remaining prepainted trim pieces.
40. Install washbasin and faucet.
41. Install toilet.
42. Finish tub and shower plumbing.
43. Install light fixtures and finish installing electrical fixtures.
44. Install towel bars and other accessories.
45. Install flooring if this has not already been done.
46. Clean up and remove trash.
47. Touch up paint and stains.
48. Test electrical and plumbing systems.
49. Obtain final inspections.
50. Move in.

Once you have established the sequence of construction, estimate the time needed to complete each step. Transfer this information to a calendar or make the sequence list into a time line by writing in the starting and ending date for each job. Some jobs can be done simultaneously, and others must be done in sequence. Contact suppliers to find out the lead times for delivery of cabinets, plumbing fixtures, floor coverings, and tile, so that you will know when to order them. Some of these items will take only a few days. Others may take months if they are shipped from overseas or must be custom-made. If a supplier requires a deposit before ordering materials, have the receipt specify that the deposit is refundable if delivery is not met by a given date. Adjust the time line to coordinate it with the delivery of the various materials. This will give you an estimated time of completion and a set of milestones along the way with which to check your progress. If you hire a contractor, you may have to coordinate the time line with his or her schedule as well.

*Opposite: Plan the details of the new bathroom with the same care you used in picking out the major fixtures. Coordinated wallpaper, ceramic tile around the tub, resilient sheet vinyl flooring, and accessories give a finished air to this room.*

# WORKING WITH PROFESSIONALS

There are many types of professionals who can help you to design, build, or remodel your bathroom. Architects, interior designers, and bathroom designers should be consulted early in the project when their expertise is most valuable. Don't forget, however, that if you are not doing the construction work yourself, it is an excellent idea to consult with the professionals who will be doing it.

## To Hire or Not to Hire

Before you engage professional help, decide to what extent you will be involved in the project. After reading this book you will have a good idea of what skills, tools, and experience are required at each stage. There is no guarantee that doing any of the work yourself will save you money, especially if you place a monetary value on your time. But if you enjoy physical work, have safe and reliable work habits, and take pleasure in shaping your own living space, you should do as much of the work as possible.

If you plan to do some of the work yourself, inventory your own tools. Organize them for quick access.

*Design professionals often have access to interesting fixtures. This toilet is trimmed in 14-karat gold leaf. You can hire a professional to do the complete design or consult one on the layout and choice of materials.*

Replace broken tools and sharpen dull ones. Mark them if there will be other people working at the site. Buy safety goggles, gloves, and dust masks. Check ladders and extension cords for safety. Schedule breaks when you can get away from the project. Prepare family members for the disruption, and above all maintain a sense of humor. Do all of these things ahead of time and you will find that the job will go much more smoothly.

## Design Professionals

An architect is trained in structural planning and in the overall arrangement of space. Unless you expect to move major walls or to make other substantial alterations, you probably won't need an architect.

Interior designers normally work with surfaces and finish materials, but many are qualified to help plan interior changes as well and can assist with other phases of the project.

A bathroom designer is a specialist. He or she may own an independent firm, or may work for a dealer who sells bathroom fixtures and supplies. As a specialist, a bathroom designer is knowledgeable about specific products and developments in the field. Some are designated as CBD, which signifies membership in the Society of Certified Bathroom Designers, under the auspices of the National Kitchen and Bath Association. Membership is based on professional experience, training, and a qualifying examination.

Designers have different ways of structuring their fees. Some work for a fixed hourly rate. Others may

charge a flat fee for designing the entire bathroom. Still others may charge a percentage of the total construction cost or a percentage of the cost of certain fixtures and supplies.

## Construction Professionals

A general contractor oversees the remodeling work. He or she is responsible for completing the project as specified in the plans. Some contractors offer design services as well, so that the entire project is handled under one roof. A general contractor hires the subcontractors and supervises their work.

Unless you are highly accomplished at home remodeling and repairs, you will need the expertise of a plumber to reroute pipes or to add new fixtures.

An electrician will rough in new wiring, add circuits, install wiring for a whirlpool, and install the finish fixtures and outlets.

A carpenter is responsible for all woodworking, including the repair or replacement of the subfloor and the installation of finish trim. A cabinetmaker can build cabinets or storage units to your specifications.

Depending on your design you may also need to contract with tile setters, glass block installers, wallpaper hangers, and other construction professionals. These specialists may be independent contractors, or they may work for the suppliers who sell these products.

In some states virtually all contractors must be licensed. In others, almost none are. In some states only one of the company's principals or managers must hold a license in order for the entire company to be considered licensed. The business may then hire any number of licensed or unlicensed individuals to perform the work. Therefore, although a license may be necessary, other qualities, such as experience and the recommendations of satisfied clients, are just as important.

## Questions to Ask Yourself

The following questions will help you to assess your own readiness for taking on various levels of involvement. For best results, be truthful and answer each question fully.

### Managing the Project

You may want to manage the job yourself and hire subcontractors to do the actual work. Although you will be hiring professionals, you will still have certain responsibilities.

Are you well organized, persistent, and clear about the details of your design? Are you free to spend time on the telephone and at the job? Can you handle money, make payments promptly, and keep a budget? Are you comfortable negotiating with subcontractors and suppliers? Are you articulate, firm, and patient? Are you willing to be friendly but to stay out of the way? Are you able to direct all inquiries, complaints, or compliments to the person with whom you signed the relevant contract—not to that person's employees?

Subcontractors depend on accurate scheduling. If your job is not ready when they arrive, they will have to reschedule it, and you may not see them again for days or even weeks. Keep all the subcontractors informed if you anticipate delays.

If you plan to hire salaried workers or unlicensed professionals who are not members of your own family, are you willing to take on the responsibilities of an employer? These responsibilities include reporting wages to the IRS, withholding state and federal taxes, paying the employer's share of those taxes, and carrying a Worker's Compensation insurance policy.

### Performing a Trade

You may want to perform one or more of the construction trades.

Are you experienced in a trade, such as carpentry or wiring, or with a material, such as wallboard, paint, or tile? Do you have access to the proper tools? Are you willing to be assigned as subcontractor by the contractor, and can you make yourself available on demand, have your materials ready, and complete the work as scheduled? If so, you can cut costs by doing some jobs yourself. You could do the work of the most highly paid professionals (usually plumbers and electricians), if you have the skills. You could do the tasks that have a high labor cost relative to the materials cost, such as wallboard finishing, insulating, and painting. And, any small jobs that would take a subcontractor less than half a day to perform, such as installing resilient sheet flooring, could be done by you.

### Doing General Labor

You, or members of your family, may want to consider doing general labor on your project. General labor is a good entry-level position into the construction trades. You may want to plan your project for summer so that high-school or college students might participate.

Is there a significant amount of demolition, hauling, or simple alterations that you could do before the professionals take over? Are you available on short notice to assist with menial tasks? Can it be clearly specified in the contract which tasks are the contractor's responsibility and which are yours? Are you in good physical condition? Do you mind getting dirty?

### Doing Everything Yourself

Doing the entire job yourself can be time consuming and frustrating, but it can also be highly satisfying. Do you enjoy working on your home? Do you have the time? Will the project disrupt normal day-to-day living? Will it matter if the project remains unfinished for several weeks? Have you finished every project you ever started? Will other family members participate or support your doing everything yourself?

# Hiring Contractors

Finding the right contractor is just as important as choosing the right bathtub or estimating costs. You may already be working with a design firm that provides contracting or installation services, or you may have selected a contractor whose work you know. Otherwise you should solicit the names of contractors from your friends and neighbors; from your designer; and from suppliers, trade associations, and other local sources.

The time-honored way to select a contractor is through competitive bidding, but bathroom remodeling does not always lend itself to fixed bids because there are so many variables. Going with the lowest bid does not guarantee that you will be satisfied with the quality of the service. Provide detailed plans and specifications; distinguish clearly between your role and that of the contractor; and set clear terms for the writing of change orders. All this will help to reduce the number of variables and make fixed-bid contracts go more smoothly. You may also consider negotiating a time-and-materials contract. The advantages of such a contract are that you pay only the actual cost of the job, and you get more attentive service. The disadvantages are that you don't know exactly how much the job will cost until it is finished, and you don't know what it would have cost to have another contractor do the same job. The main thing to recognize is that you are shopping for a unique

*Opposite: The rough-hewn granite slab countertop; the columns; and the patina on the mirror, sconces, and exposed pipes lend an ancient look to this recently remodeled bathroom. Finding new fixtures that work with older architectural styles can take some time, but it is certainly worth the effort when it is done as well as this.*

service, not a product. It isn't like shopping for an automobile.

If you solicit fixed bids, the following guidelines will help you to observe the proper etiquette.

☐ Do not solicit a formal bid if you already have a contractor in mind. Just negotiate directly.

☐ In your initial phone call to each contractor, describe the project briefly and mention that complete plans are available.

☐ Have ready a list of questions. Ask about the contractor's experience with similar projects and about his or her method of scheduling construction. Remember to ask for references.

☐ Check references by visiting job sites and completed projects. Ask previous clients if they were satisfied with the contractor's performance and attitude.

☐ Narrow down your choices to three or four people and provide each one with a complete set of plans.

☐ Set a firm date for receiving bids. Allow at least two weeks if the project is a complete remodel that will involve several subcontractors.

☐ Specify what materials and labor you yourself intend to provide.

☐ If a bidder requests clarification or further information, answer the request in writing. Send each bidder a copy of your answers, labeled Addendum. Be sure to date it.

☐ Use the same process to notify bidders of changes that you make in the plans after they have been submitted for bids.

☐ Along with the price quote, request bank or credit references and a copy of the contract form that the bidder expects you to sign.

☐ Review all of the bids and forms carefully.

The selection of a contractor should be based on several factors: personal rapport, experience with similar jobs, references and recommendations, schedules (yours and the contractor's), and cost. The low bid is not necessarily the one to choose. It may indicate poor work, inadequate supervision, or serious oversights, and it may lead to costly changes

later on. It is unethical to negotiate simultaneously with two contractors after you have received their bids, or to invite another contractor to compete after the bidding process has closed. Remember to notify all parties of your choice and of the winning bid price, and thank everybody for taking the time to bid.

## Signing the Contract

Always insist on a well-written contract. It does not have to be elaborate. Most contractors already have their own contract form; you can use that as a starting point. A good contract should include the following provisions although not all of them will apply to your particular situation.

☐ Reference to the construction documents as the criteria of performance

☐ A stipulation that the contractor is responsible for obtaining permits, performing work to code, and getting necessary inspections

☐ Specified start and completion dates and a detailed schedule

☐ A clear delineation between the contractor's supervisory duties and your own

☐ Specification of the work that you intend to perform yourself

☐ A list of all of the materials or fixtures that you will be supplying

☐ A payment schedule corresponding to key completion dates

☐ A stipulation that the contractor will provide lien releases from all subcontractors and suppliers before final payment is made

☐ Requirements for final payment, including final inspection by the building inspection department, a certificate of completion signed by you and the architect, and a 30-day waiting period

☐ A certificate of insurance from the contractor covering all risks and naming you as beneficiary

☐ A specific procedure for handling change orders

☐ Specific procedures for communication when more than one professional is involved

☐ A method for resolving disputes

# UNDERSTANDING PERMITS

*I*n most communities you will be required to obtain a building permit before you start construction. For remodeling projects, usually the homeowner is allowed to apply for the permit, but in some communities permits may be issued only to licensed contractors.

The permit will probably be issued immediately if you are making only minor alterations to an existing bathroom. If you are making major structural changes, the building inspection department may be required to check the plans, a process that could take several days.

Separate permits are customarily issued for the building, plumbing, electrical, and mechanical stages of the project.

You gain several advantages when you obtain a permit. First, of course, you have complied with the law. Second, the permit validates any work that you have done that affects the resale value of the house. Third, it decreases the possibility that an insurance company would refuse a claim against fire or other damages of dubious origin. Fourth, it gives you an incentive to plan the project thoroughly. Fifth, it instills a sense of pride in your work. Finally and most importantly, codes exist to ensure that you and your family will be living in a safe home.

## Inspections

The permit will include a schedule of inspections. Generally all work must be inspected before it is covered up. A final inspection is made after everything is hooked up and ready to go. A typical schedule of inspections appears below.

Your contractor will call for inspections and will be responsible for answering questions. However, you may have to make arrangements to let the inspector onto the premises if the contractor cannot be there.

The local building inspection department can tell you what codes pertain to your work and can answer specific questions about code requirements. However, staff members cannot tell you how to do the work. If you have done the work yourself and are not sure whether it will meet code, hire a professional who is familiar with the local codes to take a look at the job before the inspection.

## Preparing Yourself for Construction

A remodeling project inevitably causes disruptions and mess. Water turned off at the wrong time is annoying; the lack of a door, inconvenient; the loss of a bathroom for several days, nerve-wracking. The more familiar you are with the plans and the schedule, the better you will be able to cope.

Prepare as much as possible ahead of time, before you actually have to move out of the bathroom. Clear out the area where you will be working. Plan how and where debris will be piled. Collect cardboard boxes for carrying out plaster and scraps. Inquire about rental rates for a debris box or a truck. Place orders early for materials with long delivery times. Clear out the garage or some similar area where large, bulky items, such as a bathtub or a shower stall, can be stored. Decide what you will do with the old fixtures.

**Opposite:** *Though following building codes and working with inspectors may seem a cumbersome inconvenience while you're in the midst of construction, these codes were developed for your safety and the safety of your family. Remember that building "up to code" will result in a finer bathroom and a job you can be proud of for years to come.*

## Inspection Schedule

| Job | Work to Be Checked | Time of Inspection |
|---|---|---|
| Foundation | Trench, forms, rebar | Before concrete is poured |
| Under floor | Floor framing, utility lines | Before subfloor is installed |
| Framing | Grade and size of lumber, spans, connections, sheathing | Before walls are insulated or covered up |
| Rough plumbing | Pipe sizes, fittings, pressure test | Before framing is inspected or walls are covered up |
| Rough wiring | Wire size, boxes, bends | Before framing is inspected or walls are covered up |
| Rough mechanical | Ducts, flues, clearances, gas lines | Before framing is inspected or walls are covered up |
| Insulation | Thickness, joints, cracks | Before wallboard is applied |
| Interior walls | Wallboard nailing pattern (may not be required) | Before joints are taped |
| Final inspection | Electrical fixtures, plumbing fixtures, window glass, stairs | After completion |

# CONSTRUCTION GUIDE

Remodeling a bathroom is a demanding project, one that requires careful preparation, close coordination, and accurate work. It calls for many different skills and a variety of materials and fixtures. It will probably mean having to get along without the bathroom for a few days—possibly even for several weeks. For most homeowners, however, the reward of a beautiful new bathroom and the satisfaction of having improved their home offset any inconveniences. Whether you are doing all of the work yourself, hiring a contractor to do all of it, or doing some of the work yourself and engaging professionals to do the rest, this chapter will guide you through each phase of the project, from demolition through finishing techniques. Tasks that are unique to bathroom remodeling, such as removing a bathtub or installing a toilet, are presented in complete step-by-step detail. Tasks that are common to all types of remodeling, such as framing walls, installing electrical wiring, or finishing plasterboard, are summarized briefly.

*Constructing a new bathroom or remodeling an existing room requires the same expertise. Remodeling, however, adds steps to the building process. Allow plenty of time to demolish or remove existing fixtures before you begin the new construction.*

# PREPARING FOR CONSTRUCTION

*There are several things you can do before you begin construction that will make the work go more easily. The first is to arrange for the use of a bathroom during the remodeling. If you are fortunate enough to have a second bathroom, you will suffer only minor inconvenience while remodeling. If you are remodeling the only bathroom in the house, you have three options.*

One option is to try to phase the project in such a way that at least the toilet and possibly the bathtub will be functional at all times. If you are hiring professionals to do all the work, this approach may be more expensive, and you will probably have access to the bathroom only in the morning and evenings anyway. Remember that the workers will need to have the use of a bathroom during the day, however, and that there may be one or two days when all of the fixtures are out of order no matter how well you have planned the project. Then you must revert to the second option, which is to rent or borrow temporary facilities. Consider renting a portable toilet or a recreational vehicle with a bathroom for the duration of the project or relying on neighbors, friends, or family for the use of their bathroom while yours is out of commission. Taking a vacation while your bathroom is being remodeled is the third option.

## Tools

Construction goes much more smoothly when you have the right tools. Most tasks can be done with basic hand tools, but be sure that they are of good quality, and do not hesitate to buy a tool you don't have. There is no substitute for the right tool. Depending on the scope of the work, you will need a hammer with a ripping claw, a utility knife with extra blades, a flat pry bar, a demolition or cold chisel, a 3-inch-wide putty knife, a minihacksaw, a small handsaw, an adjustable wrench, adjustable pliers, pipe wrenches, an assortment of screwdrivers, a framing square, and a simple voltage tester. More specialized tools include needle-nose pliers, side cutters, end cutters, a large crowbar, a brickset, a basin wrench, a sledgehammer, a maul, and a flat shovel for loading debris. Power tools that are helpful include a reciprocating saw with both long and short blades, a ⅜-inch drill with screwdriver bits (cordless if you are purchasing a new one), and a circular saw with carbide tipped blades.

## Safety

Always think safety first at any construction site. Because a bathroom is so small, it may not seem like a construction site, but the potential hazards are the same. Safe work habits, a minimum of clutter, basic safety equipment, and an awareness of your own limitations will greatly reduce your chances of being injured. Have gloves, safety goggles, dust masks, and a hard hat available at all times, and use them whenever the situation calls for it. Get a tetanus shot if you have not had one recently.

Observe safe work habits. Don't try to force things; let your tools do the work. Wear a hard hat whenever someone is working above you or whenever you are removing ceiling materials. Be aware of safe lifting techniques: Use your legs instead of your back; keep a firm footing; and avoid twisting your back as you lift or hold heavy objects. Before you toss boards on the debris pile, always remove any nails or bend them flat. Wear a particle mask or a respirator during dusty operations. If you encounter asbestos (that is rare in the bathroom, but it may be present in some flooring materials), seek professional assistance. Read directions carefully for solvents, adhesives, and other flammable products. Avoid working when you are physically or mentally fatigued and be extra alert toward the end of the day. Injuries often occur around quitting time.

Use power tools with care. Make sure that the safety guards are intact; wear goggles; and do not wear loose clothing. Be sure that electrical cords and tools are in good condition and are properly grounded. Keep saw blades and drill bits sharp.

Turn off the circuit breakers or disconnect the fuses that serve the wires in the area where you will be working. Cover the breaker with tape to warn other people that it was turned off intentionally. Use a voltage tester to double-check all the wires in electrical outlets or fixtures that you plan to work on. When in doubt, consult an electrician.

It is not likely that you will be working on gas appliances in a bathroom. Nor are you likely to encounter gas lines unless there is a common wall between the kitchen and the bathroom or unless there is a gas water heater nearby. However, if you

*Opposite: As daily exercise becomes more popular, people need room for their exercise equipment. This former bedroom is now used as a combination spa and gym.*

do inadvertently disconnect a gas line, be prepared to shut off the main gas valve immediately. In most houses the main valve is next to the gas meter, and you will need a wrench to turn it. Once you have shut off the gas to the whole house, the pilot lights for any gas appliances without electronic ignition, such as older furnaces, water heaters, and ranges, will have to be relit. It is a good idea to have a service representative from the utility company come out and help you when you are ready to turn the gas back on and to relight the pilots.

## Logistics

Decide now how you will deal with debris and where you will store materials. Even a modest bathroom project can generate a mountain of trash in no time. You can haul everything away as you remove it (which requires a pickup truck, a trailer, or a large station wagon); you can pile the debris in an inconspicuous but convenient spot and have it hauled away at the end of the job; or you can rent a debris box and toss the trash into it as you go. Most debris box services require pickup within a week, so

within that time you will have to complete the demolition. In any case, there will be more debris later.

Make arrangements for storing fixtures or cabinets that you plan to reuse, as well as new materials that may be delivered before you need them. Some materials can be stored outside under a tarp, but others, such as cabinets and wallboard, must be stored in a dry, covered area. A large, empty garage with easy driveway access or an empty room inside the house is ideal. Also designate a convenient and well-organized area for storing tools.

# DEMOLISHING THE EXISTING ROOM

**I**t is easy to think of demolition as sledgehammer work, but it seldom requires brute strength. You will be more successful if you think of it as finesse work, taking things a step at a time and nibbling away at the bathroom rather than trying to demolish everything at once.

Even if you are moving walls or making structural changes, it may encourage you to know that demolition requires more common sense than technical skill and knowledge of a few fundamentals rather than a specific answer to every question that comes up. Planning the job carefully, having the proper tools, and developing safe work habits will do more to ensure a successful project than simply having the appropriate skills and techniques.

Before you begin work, seal off all doorways and passages to keep dust and debris out of the rest of the house. Shut any doors that can be left closed. Then apply duct tape all around the edges, and especially around the bottom, sticking the tape to the door and also to the floor. For doors that must remain in use, apply duct tape along the bottom on both sides, sticking it to the door but not to the floor. It will act as a dust sweep as you open and close the door. Passageways without doors can be sealed with 4-mil plastic sheeting. Attach it to the ceiling with a 1 by 2 or similar board, driving the nails into the ceiling joists. Use another board to anchor the bottom to the floor. With the bathroom cleared out and sealed off from the rest of the house, you are now ready to begin the demolition. First, however, lay a trail of drop cloths or sheets of cardboard between the bathroom and the outdoors, and between the bathroom door and the adjacent rooms. This will help to protect the landscaping, as well as the floors in other parts of the house.

Start the demolition process by taking out all the little accessories attached here and there. These include the towel bars, soap dish, toothbrush holder, light fixtures, and window treatments. Be especially careful with anything that you intend to save; find a space well away from the construction site to store these things. Next remove the easiest and least necessary items; these are usually the ones that do not involve plumbing. Remove the plumbing fixtures last. You might even wait to take the fixtures out until the new units are ready to install, especially if you will be using the bathroom during construction.

## Removing Shelves and Storage Units

Shelving units are relatively easy to dismantle. Detach them from the wall, either by unscrewing the fasteners that hold them in place or by gently prying them from the wall with a flat bar. If the shelf is sealed to the wall with many layers of paint, use a utility knife to score through the seal. If you intend to save the wall, place a flat shim, such as a piece of ½-inch plywood, between the wall and the pry bar to prevent the bar from gouging the wall.

Some bathrooms have prefabricated storage units much like kitchen cabinets that can be removed in one piece and saved. Open the unit and look for the screws on the back panel that hold it to the wall. Unscrew them and remove the cabinet. In most older bathrooms the storage cabinets were built in place and must be dismantled. Start by taking out the drawers, doors, and shelves. Then try to determine how the unit was constructed and work backwards, removing the pieces first that were installed last. Knock each piece loose with a hammer, pry it out, or cut it off with a saw.

To remove a surface-mounted medicine cabinet, start by scoring around the edge to break the paint seal. Then look inside for the screws that hold the cabinet to the wall. The screws may be covered with paint, so look for telltale depressions near each corner. Scrape off the paint and unscrew them. The cabinet should come loose. If it is held with nails, gently pry the whole cabinet from the wall or pull the nails from the inside with a cat's paw and a hammer.

A flush-mounted medicine cabinet is usually held in place with screws on the two sides. Remove them and pull the cabinet out of the wall cavity. Old wooden cabinets may have to be dismantled piece by piece, starting with the door.

## Removing Washbasins

Washbasins may be wall mounted, freestanding, or set into a countertop. Removal is similar for all three types. The task can usually be done by one person, although you may need help to remove a wall-mounted cast-iron basin. Turn off the water supply at the shutoff valves below the sink. In rare cases there may be no shutoff valves; turn off the water at the main house valve. Leave the faucet in the basin and remove the whole thing as one unit. You can remove the faucet later if you intend to reuse it or the basin. Have handy a bucket or a dishpan that will fit under the shutoff valves and the P-trap.

1. Disconnect the plumbing. First place the bucket or dishpan under the shutoff valves and disconnect the water supply lines (the vertical tubes) with an adjustable wrench. Open the sink faucet to allow any water trapped in the lines to drain into the bucket. If there are no shutoff valves, disconnect the water pipes from the faucet. Use a basin wrench to reach

up underneath the basin and unscrew the connecting nuts, or use a hacksaw to cut through the old pipes; you will want to replace them and install proper shutoff valves anyway. Place a bucket under the P-trap and loosen the slip nuts with a pair of slip-joint pliers. Finish unscrewing them by hand and drop the trap into the bucket.

2. To remove a wall-mounted basin, look underneath it for the bolts or screws that secure it to the mounting bracket. Remove them. Then, with a helper, lift the basin straight up until it clears the mounting bracket and set it aside. Remove the screws that hold the mounting bracket to the wall and take it off.

3. There are two types of pedestal basin. The first type is simply a wall-mounted sink with a pedestal placed under it for decoration. Look for any bolts or screws that secure the pedestal to the floor and remove them. Then slide the pedestal out carefully and remove the sink in the same way as any other wall-mounted model. The second type of pedestal basin is completely supported by the pedestal, so remove the sink first—there may be screws or bolts holding it to the wall and to the pedestal—and then remove the pedestal.

4. A basin set into a countertop can be removed separately or along with the counter. If you remove it separately, the technique you use will depend on whether the rim is mounted above or below the surface of the counter. The simplest installations are basins with integral rims that rest on the countertop. Pry under the rim with a flat bar to loosen it and then lift out the basin. In a similar but more complicated installation, a surface-mounted metal rim holds the basin in place with special clips installed from below. Loosen the clips with a screwdriver and remove them. The basin will drop down as soon as you do this, so if it is heavy or fragile, secure it first with a rope and 2 by 4s.

If countertop material covers the rim of the basin, or if it is installed flush with the rim, you will have to remove the countertop before you take out the basin. If it is a tile counter, chip away the trim pieces that lock the basin rim in place. Use a hammer and chisel. Wear gloves and goggles; broken tile is very sharp. If the countertop is a solid slab of cultured marble or similar material, remove it in one piece before you take out the basin.

## Removing Countertops and Vanities

1. Remove the doors and drawers from the vanity. Then look inside for the fastening brackets, screws, or other devices that hold the countertop in place. Unscrew them and remove the countertop. Some slab counters are attached to the vanity only by a bead of caulk. Working from above, slide a putty knife or scraper between the slab and the vanity to break the seal. This will prevent the slab from snapping when you pry it off. Then pry the countertop loose around the edges with a flat bar and lift it away.

2. Tile countertops may have a plywood base that was nailed or screwed to the vanity from above before the tile was installed. This base cannot be reached without demolishing the tile. To avoid the extra effort that this would entail, try to remove the countertop in one piece by prying it up and away from the vanity—or remove the vanity with the countertop still attached.

3. Remove any screws holding the vanity to the wall. They are usually located along the top rail. Then slide the vanity forward, lifting it clear of the flooring, and carry it away.

## Removing Toilets

Taking out a toilet may seem like a complicated job. Actually it is quite simple. In fact, it can be done by one person; the hardest part is lifting out the fixture and carrying it away.

1. If you are salvaging the toilet or the toilet seat, remove the seat and lid by unscrewing the nuts that hold them in place. Then turn off the water supply to the toilet. Remove the tank lid. Flush the toilet until both the bowl and the tank are empty, and sponge up any remaining water.

2. Disconnect the water supply line by unscrewing the retaining nut at the bottom of the tank or the coupling nut at the shutoff valve. Unscrew both if you wish to remove the supply tubing. Cover the exposed outlet of the shutoff valve with tape to prevent dust and debris from falling in. To make it easier to lift out the bowl, first remove the tank. Unscrew the two or three nuts that hold the tank to the bowl and lift it off. Some old toilets have a wall-mounted tank connected to the bowl by an L-shaped pipe. Remove the pipe first by unscrewing the coupling nuts and any retaining bolts. Remove the bolts that hold the tank to the wall and set the tank aside.

3. To remove the bowl, pry off the plastic or ceramic caps that cover the closet bolts and remove the nuts with a small wrench. Rock the bowl gently back and forth to loosen it from the wax seal around the drain flange. Lift it up carefully. A considerable amount of water will be left in the drain trap. Set the toilet in the tub or shower and tip it to drain this water out before you carry the toilet through the house. Place old towels in the bottom of the tub or shower to keep the toilet from scratching it.

4. Slide the closet bolts out of the slots in the exposed drain flange and scrape away the old wax seal with a putty knife. If you intend to install a new toilet in the same place, inspect the flange for cracks or other damage and replace it if necessary. Temporarily seal the drainpipe opening with rags, duct tape, or an expansion plug to keep debris out and to keep sewer gas from entering the house.

## Removing Floor Coverings

It is not always necessary to remove the old floor covering in order to install a new one. But you must remove it if the subfloor is damaged and needs to be repaired. Otherwise it depends on the nature and the condition of the finish floor. If the existing floor covering is linoleum or vinyl that is in good condition and free of wax or polish, many kinds of flooring can be laid directly over it. If it is cracked and uneven, you may be able to patch it; otherwise install a plywood or hardboard underlayment over it and install the new flooring on top of that. New tile may require a structural underlayment to stiffen the floor. The old floor covering should be removed if laying new flooring over it will raise the level of the floor too high. This can happen if there is more than one layer of flooring, if the finish floor is installed over an underlayment, or if tile was installed over a mortar bed. The old flooring should also be removed if the new flooring or underlayment cannot be made to adhere to it. See page 105 for more information about installing flooring.

1. To remove the old floor covering, begin by prying off any baseboards that cover it at the edges. If you expect to reuse the baseboard, score the joint between it and the wall with a utility knife to break the paint seal. Then pry off the baseboard gently. If it resists, drive the finishing nails completely through it with a nail set and

lift it free. If any nails are left in the baseboard after you remove it, pull them out with pliers. Work from the back so as not to mar the finished surface. To remove rubber or vinyl base coving, run a 3-inch-wide putty knife behind it and pry it loose.

2. Remove linoleum or vinyl tiles by prying them up, one by one, using a wide pry bar, a putty knife, a chisel, or a floor scraper. Sometimes they will pop right out. Usually the mastic is very strong, and you are in for a tedious, time-consuming job. The backing on some older tiles contains asbestos fibers that are released into the air when the tiles are broken or jarred. Consult with a local environmental agency if you suspect that there is asbestos in your flooring. They will tell you what precautions you should take and what legal requirements you must meet. At the

very least you should wear safety goggles, gloves, and a respirator designated for asbestos, and you should dispose of the broken pieces in air tight plastic bags. Depending on the type of material, it may be necessary to have the flooring removed by a licensed asbestos contractor.

3. Remove sheet vinyl or linoleum following the procedures outlined above under Step 2. The job will be easier if you slice the flooring into small sections with a utility knife first. Pry up the sections and scrape off any mastic that remains on the floor.

4. Resilient flooring, whether sheet or tile, may have been installed over an underlayment of plywood, hardboard, or other similar material. If so, it is much easier to pull up the underlayment and flooring together than it is to remove just the flooring. First cut the underlayment into sections 3 or

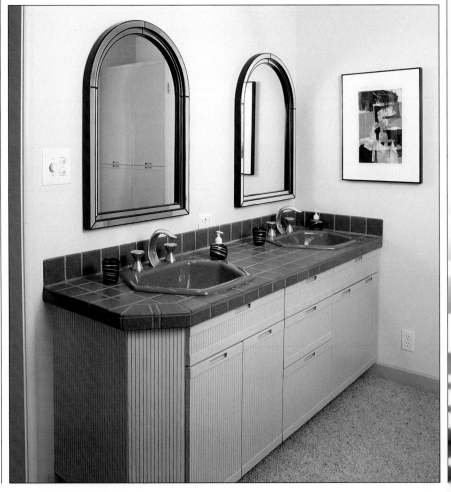

*A good rule of thumb in combining colors is to keep most items within one color range, such as the gray tones shown here, and then select one accent item—the mauve sinks—to really stand out.*

4 feet square. Use a circular saw with an old carbide blade—you will probably hit nails—and set the blade depth so that it will just cut through the underlayment without cutting into the subfloor. Then pry up the sections of underlayment and flooring together and discard them.

5. Remove ceramic tile with a hammer and a wide chisel. A brickset works very well. To remove the first tile, break it into pieces and chip them out. Then force the chisel underneath the adjacent whole tiles and pop them up. Wear gloves and goggles. Broken tile is very sharp.

If the tile floor was installed over a mortar bed, it is usually easier to force up the mortar than it is to remove the individual tiles. Use a large crowbar or a pickax to pry underneath the mortar bed. Alternately lift on the bar and hammer down next to it with a sledgehammer. When the bed cracks, it may expose reinforcing wires. Cut them with wire cutters and remove each section. Work carefully to avoid injuring yourself or damaging the subfloor. In most cases an old mortar bed extends down between the floor joists, where it is supported by boards laid over cleats nailed to the sides of the joists. Sometimes the joists have been tapered at the top, in which case you must attach 2 by 4 nailers on both sides of each joist, flush with the top, to support a new subfloor.

It is sometimes possible to install resilient sheet flooring over ceramic tile. The tile must be in good condition. Roughen it first by sanding it with coarse abrasive paper. Then attach a plywood underlayment to the tile, using construction glue and a caulking gun.

## Removing Lights and Electrical Fixtures

You can remove lights and other fixtures during the demolition process or when the rough wiring is being installed. It depends on what other work is being done. You will need to remove the lights if you are removing the wall or ceiling materials around them, if you are changing their location, or if you are doing extensive rewiring. If you are simply changing the light fixtures, however, you need not remove the old ones until you install the new ones. To remove any kind of electrical fixture, first turn off the circuit breakers for the bathroom area and put tape over the handles so that no one turns them back on.

1. Most bathroom light fixtures are surface-mounted ceiling or wall units with some kind of globe. Remove the globe and the light bulb. Then loosen the screws that hold the housing to the electrical box inside the wall or ceiling. Gently pull the housing out far enough to expose the wiring. Disconnect the fixture wires from the house wires and remove the fixture. Cap the house wires with wire nuts and push them all back into the electrical box.

2. To remove a fluorescent fixture, first take out the tube. Then loosen the screws or nuts that hold the cover in place and lift it away to expose the wires. Disconnect the fixture wires from the house wires, unless the connection is made inside the electrical box. In that case remove the fixture housing by loosening the circular

*Consider a greenhouse window to expand the space and increase the light within a bathroom. These windows are fairly easy to install, and most of them fit standard openings. The shower door features an original piece of art that has been etched onto the tempered glass.*

locknut from the hollow stud that the wires go through; pull the housing away from the wall or ceiling; and disconnect the wires. Cap the house wires and push them back into the electrical box.

3. Remove all the covers from the electrical outlets and switches. This will make it easier to demolish the wall and ceiling materials. The fixtures themselves can be left in place until they are moved or replaced when installing new wiring.

## Removing Wall and Ceiling Materials

It may not be necessary to take out any wall or ceiling materials. You may be able to paint or wallpaper the old surfaces. However, if the walls and ceiling are in poor shape, or if you intend to alter the structure, the wiring, or the plumbing, then some of the surface materials must be removed. If you are only providing access for small changes in the plumbing and wiring, you can wait until later to make the openings—but be ready for surprises.

Removing wall and ceiling materials can be messy and time-consuming, but it is not particularly complicated. Wear gloves, goggles, a dust mask, and a hard hat when you are removing plaster or plasterboard. Turn off the electrical circuits near the walls that you are working on, and work carefully to avoid hitting wires, pipes, or ducts inside the walls. If the project is a complete renovation with extensive structural, wiring, and plumbing alterations, gut the room to the wall studs and ceiling framing. It is tempting to leave small sections of wall or ceiling material intact, but they are seldom worth saving—it is tedious to patch into them, and you will probably need to get behind them to work on the wiring or insulation anyway.

Remove ceramic wall tiles in the same way as you remove floor tiles (see page 79).

### Trim

Remove the trim first. If you plan to save it, score along the edge of each piece with a utility knife. Then pry it off the wall with a flat bar, working gently, and pull the nails out through the back with a pair of end cutters. Mark each piece so that you will know later where it goes.

### Wallcoverings

To remove a single layer of the wallcovering, spray it with wallpaper remover, one section at a time. Let the solution set, respray, and peel off each section with a wide putty knife. Start from the floor and work upward at an angle. To remove several layers, rent a steamer or hire professional help. After the wallcovering is off, wash down the wall with a sponge and a weak solution of trisodium phosphate (TSP), rinse, and let dry. Then sand any uneven areas.

### Plasterboard

First cut a clean line all around the section that you intend to remove. If this section includes a corner, cut through the joint tape with a utility knife. If demolition is to stop in the middle of a wall or a ceiling, make the cut down the center of a stud or a joist. Use a hammer and chisel, a sharp utility knife, or a circular saw set to the depth of the plasterboard. Sawing will kick up a lot of dust; chiseling or scoring is more tedious but cleaner. Do not worry about making a perfectly straight line. Now tear the plasterboard off the framing in large chunks, using a ripping hammer, a wrecking bar, or your hands. Always pull; never push. Wear gloves, a dust mask, and goggles. Wear a hard hat if you are tearing out the ceiling; dust and insulation will come cascading down. Watch out for wires and utility lines hidden behind the walls. Pull the nails as you go.

To remove a small section of plasterboard, lay out the guidelines with a framing square. The top and bottom lines should be level. The side lines should be centered over studs. To

mark the studs, knock a small hole in the center of the proposed opening and insert a tape measure through the hole, horizontally, until the end reaches a stud. Transfer this measurement to the surface of the wall, add ¾ inch (half the thickness of the stud), and make a mark on the wall. This mark indicates the center of the stud. Repeat the operation for the stud on the other side. To cut, use a drywall saw or a reciprocating saw between the studs and make repeated passes with a utility knife where the line passes over a stud.

### Lath and Plaster

Use a hammer and chisel to score a break line at the point where the demolition will end. Tap gently but firmly. Strip the plaster from the lath with the claw of a ripping hammer or a hooked wrecking bar. When the plaster is off, remove the lath a piece at a time. If the end of a lath is locked into a corner, rock it up and down, not side to side, to work it free.

Making smaller openings requires careful work to avoid jarring loose the adjacent plaster. First lay out guidelines. Center them over studs (to find the studs, probe with a hammer and nail). Then cut along the lines with a hammer and chisel and remove the plaster. Use a hammer and a sharp chisel to cut through the lath where it crosses the studs. If you are cutting lath between the studs, use a keyhole saw, bearing heavily on the push stroke and lightly on the pull stroke. It is also messy but possible to cut through lath and plaster with a circular saw. Use a carbide-tipped blade set to the depth of the lath and run the saw firmly and slowly. Loose lath can bind the blade, so be ready for kickbacks.

**Opposite:** *Dimensioned-stone tile lends an elegant look to any room. Stone tile—granite, marble, or slate—is installed in the same way as ceramic tile.*

## Removing Bathtubs

The bathtub is the hardest of all bathroom fixtures to remove. For this reason it is usually saved until last. It is large and often very heavy, and the plumbing may be hard to reach. If the tub is a freestanding claw-foot model, you can probably get to the plumbing quite easily. However, if the tub is built into an alcove or a corner, you will need to gain access to the back of the plumbing wall. You will also have to remove the tile or trim around the rim. In any case, you will need at least two helpers.

1. Remove the shower doors and their frame, if installed. Some doors can be removed simply by lifting them off the tracks. To remove others, you must raise the top bar slightly while a helper lifts each door out of the bottom track. When the doors are out, lift the top bar completely free of the frame. Remove the side and bottom bars by unscrewing them or by prying them loose.

2. Turn off the water to the tub. Some bathtubs have shutoff valves located behind a door or a removable panel on the backside of the end wall. If there are no shutoff valves,

turn off the water at the main valve.

3. If there is no removable panel behind the end wall, cut an opening to provide access to the drainpipes. Lay out the cut so that the sides are centered over studs, the bottom is about 2 inches above the floor or the baseboard, and the top is slightly above the rim of the tub. To cut, use the techniques on page 80.

4. Disconnect the drain by unscrewing the coupling nut at the top of the P-trap. With the nut loosened, the tub drainpipe should separate from the P-trap when the tub is lifted slightly, making it unnecessary to remove

the entire drain and overflow assembly. If it is impossible to lift the tub, or if the drain and overflow assembly will get in the way as you slide the tub out, remove it. From the finished side of the tub, disassemble the overflow cover and the stopper mechanism and take them out. Then remove the screws that hold the overflow pipe in place. Now, working from behind the tub, loosen the coupling nuts that hold the overflow pipe and the drain elbow in place. The overflow pipe should come out. If you have to remove the drain elbow as well, work from inside the tub. Insert a special plumber's tool that resembles a fork into the crosspiece of the drain and unscrew it, using a screwdriver or heavy-duty pliers to twist the tool. (If you do not have this special tool, you can improvise, using the handle of a pair of pliers.) If the fitting resists, wait until the tub is out. Then use a wrench to grip the bottom side of the fitting at the same time as you twist the top side.

5. Remove the faucet handles and the spout. If the tub is a freestanding claw-foot model, disconnect the water supply lines from the faucet and remove the tub from the bathroom. You will need two or three helpers and a dolly.

6. For a built-in tub, remove enough of the wallcovering to expose the top of the rim. Use the techniques described on page 80. If the tub has flanges anchored to the wall with screws or nails, remove them.

7. Using a pry bar and working with several helpers, raise one end of the tub until you can slide a 1-by or 2-by runner beneath it. Do the same thing with the other end. Slide the tub out of the alcove, set it on a dolly,

*Opposite: Removing existing fixtures need not always mean disposing of them completely. This antique makes an excellent soaking tub in a sun porch used as a sitting room off a master bedroom. The floor isn't really tile; it's painted wood.*

and remove it. If it won't go through the doorway, take off the door. If it still won't clear, stand the tub on end and work it through the doorway narrow side first. Lower it carefully onto the dolly when you get it outside the room. If you don't have a dolly, you can move a heavy tub on several short rollers cut from 1½-inch plastic drainpipe. Have plenty of help.

In some cases the tub may be too large or too heavy to take out at all. You can break up a cast-iron tub with a sledgehammer and remove it in pieces. Also, you can cut a steel tub in half, using a reciprocating saw with a hacksaw blade.

## Removing Shower Stalls

Whether you plan to refurbish the existing shower stall or remove it completely, it should be gutted all the way down to the studs. You may want to leave the shower pan in place if it is in good condition and if it harmonizes with the new tile. Otherwise take it out too.

1. Remove the shower door by unscrewing the hinges or the channel that supports it. Then dismantle the rest of the frame. Some pieces may be held in place by screws. Other pieces may be held by caulk or putty; these pieces can be pried out or knocked free.

2. Remove the faucet handles and the showerhead.

3. Remove the wallcovering. If the stall is a plastic or fiberglass unit, remove enough of the plasterboard to expose the flanges around the top. Remove the nails holding the flanges in place and pry out the stall in sections. Wear gloves and goggles. If you wish to remove the stall in one piece, disconnect the drain first.

To remove a tile surround, especially those set in a mortar bed, take special precautions. The tile and mortar are heavy, and broken tile is very sharp. Wear thick clothing, gloves, goggles, a hard hat, and heavy shoes. Protect any nearby fixtures if you are saving them, with

heavy padded tarps, several layers of cardboard, or thick plywood. Remove the tile and mortar in sections. Start at the bottom of each section and work up. Use a heavy chisel and a maul to break the tile and mortar into pieces and a crowbar to pry the pieces off the wall.

4. To disconnect the drain for a one-piece prefabricated unit, remove the drain cover and look for a ring or other fastening device around the edge of the drain. Unscrew it and remove it, along with any gasket that it held in place. Lift the shower unit straight up to clear the floor pipe. Then pull it out. A one-piece prefabricated shower pan is removed in the same way.

5. A tiled shower pan is more difficult to remove because it is set in a mortar bed and must be broken up. Remove any framing that supports the curb. This will expose some of the mortar bed. Break away as much of it as you can. Then pry underneath the mortar bed with a large crowbar to break up the pan. Leave the drain intact until you have got out all of the mortar and tile. The drain should be replaced if you are installing a new shower in the same location. Otherwise remove it by sawing through the pipe just below floor level. Cap the open pipe to prevent sewer gas from entering the house.

6. If you are removing the shower stall completely, take out the water pipes as well. Turn off the water at the main valve and drain the pipes. To do this, first open any faucets in the house that are at a lower level than the shower pipes and then open the shower valve. Using a hacksaw and pipe wrenches, remove the pipes back to fittings that you can cap and that are out of the way.

7. Remove the studs and framing members of the partition walls. Cut through the studs at an angle so as not to bind the saw. When removing the end studs, work carefully to keep from damaging the surface of the walls in the adjoining rooms.

# MAKING STRUCTURAL IMPROVEMENTS

*T*he next step after demolition is to prepare the space for the new fixtures. This may involve anything from minor patching and touch-up to major structural, plumbing, electrical, and insulation work. It is beyond the scope of this book to cover all of the relevant techniques, but the ones that are unique to bathrooms are described.

The sequence of construction varies from project to project. One option is to finish the walls and floor before you install any fixtures. Another is to install all of the fixtures except the toilet, then lay the flooring, then install the toilet, and finally paint the room. The order depends on the extent of the project, the materials involved, and the schedules of the people who will be doing the work. You may need to flip back and forth through this chapter to order your own sequence of construction.

If the project involves adding on a room, the shell can be framed and closed in before you open up the wall and disrupt the original bathroom. However, if any plumbing, wiring, or duct work will be run under the new floor, it must be installed and inspected before you install the subflooring over the joists. You may have to alter the existing bathroom plumbing to make the connections. Plumb-

*Installing a second vanity area within the master bedroom helps to relieve the pressure when two people are trying to get ready at the same time. See page 65 for a view of the rest of this bathroom suite.*

ing vents, chimneys, flues, and ventilating ducts that penetrate the roof should be installed before the roofing goes on so that they can be flashed properly. Leave an opening in the exterior wall for removing old fixtures and debris and for delivering bulky items.

Rough framing techniques for a bathroom are the same as those for any other room and are summarized in the guidelines that follow. Start

with repairs to the floor framing and the subfloor.

## Floors

A sound floor system is the first prerequisite for a successful remodeling project. Depending on the scope of your particular job, you may need to do only simple repairs, or you may need to reinforce the entire floor.

## Repairs

Whether you install flooring now or later, the key to a good installation is preparation of the subsurface. First inspect the subfloor and the floor framing. Look for rot damage, structural weaknesses, and surface deformities. If you have removed the old finish floor, you can inspect the subfloor from above, but any structural damage to the framing may go unnoticed unless you also inspect from below. Pay close attention to the toilet and tub areas even if it means making inspection holes in a downstairs ceiling. If you find damage, repair it now, whether the flooring is installed now or later.

Subflooring that is rotted or badly damaged should be replaced. Cut out a rectangular section of subfloor around the damaged area. The cutout should extend at least 12 inches beyond any rotted wood, and the edges should be centered over floor joists. Use a circular saw with the blade set to the depth of the subflooring so that you won't cut any joists. Cut a replacement patch out of plywood of the same thickness as the subfloor. Allow $1/16$ inch to $1/8$ inch of clearance for expansion. Nail 2 by 4 blocking between the joists to support the edges of the patch. Set the patch in place and nail it to the joists and blocking with 8-penny (8d) ring-shank nails.

Floor joists and other framing members seldom need to be repaired unless the floor is sagging or decaying. Extensive structural repair will require professional help. If the damage is limited to one or two floor joists, nail a length of 2-by lumber of the same width next to the damaged joist. Attach it with 12d or 16d common nails along the top edge, along the bottom edge, and down the center. If the damage is due to rot, support both sides of the rotted section with temporary shoring and cut the section out. Then nail a new joist to the truncated joist. The new joist should be long enough to rest on the girders or other bearing members. If

this is impossible, it should be at least long enough to extend beyond the cutout 4 feet in each direction. Nail the two joists together with 12d or 16d common nails.

### Reinforcement

Bathtubs, particularly large luxury tubs or cast-iron models, can be very heavy. Ideally the tub should be located over or near a foundation wall, a girder, or a bearing wall. Otherwise, if it lies perpendicular to the joists, they will probably be strong enough to support it as long as they are properly sized for normal loads, are not weakened by notches or holes, and have end support over the foundation walls or the bearing walls.

If the tub lies parallel to the joists or if it lies perpendicular to them but is

centered over a long joist span, double up the joists under the edges of the tub or under the feet or both.

A sunken bathtub requires different floor support altogether. If the bathroom is located over a shallow crawl space, the tub should be supported by a concrete slab on the ground. If the bathroom is located over a basement or a first floor, the tub should be supported by dropped floor joists carried on bearing walls.

### Toilet

The toilet in an upstairs bathroom may need special floor framing to provide enough room for the closet bend. If a joist is in the way, cut it and support it with headers. Double the headers and the joists that support them if you have to cut more than one joist.

### Repairing a Damaged Subfloor

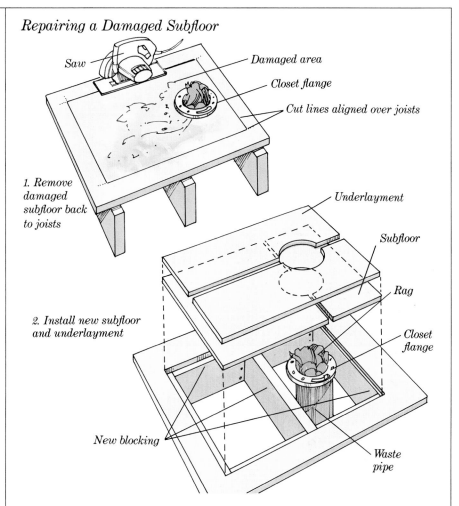

Saw

Damaged area

Closet flange

Cut lines aligned over joists

1. Remove damaged subfloor back to joists

Underlayment

Subfloor

Rag

2. Install new subfloor and underlayment

Closet flange

New blocking

Waste pipe

## Walls and Ceilings

When it comes to framing the ceiling and the walls, there are certain details that occur more often in bathrooms than in other rooms.

### Plumbing Walls

Some plumbing cannot fit inside a 2 by 4 wall. Examples include a 4-inch soil stack, fittings for a 3-inch soil stack, 2-inch cast-iron fittings, and large shower valves. To make an existing wall wide enough to accommodate plumbing, fur it out with 2 by 2s. If you are building a new wall, use 2 by 6s or 2 by 8s.

### Wing Walls

Partition walls, called wing walls or pony walls, that jut out from another wall for 2 or 3 feet are often used to enclose a bathtub, create a toilet compartment, or define the end of a vanity cabinet. If they extend all the way from floor to ceiling, wing walls can be framed like any stud wall, with the top plates tied into the ceiling joists or into blocking set between the ceiling joists.

Often a wing wall is designed to stop short of the ceiling, creating a feeling of space and admitting more natural light into an alcove. Because this type of wall has no support along the top and one entire edge, other means must be used to stabilize it.

If a cabinet, shelving, or counter will be installed against the wing wall and the adjacent wall, that alone should provide adequate support as long as the unit is well secured.

If the wing wall is freestanding, there are several ways to increase its stability. One is to assemble the framing with screws instead of nails. Another is to stiffen the wall by using ⅝-inch, rather than ½-inch, plasterboard or plywood. A third way is to anchor the front edge of the wall by using a long 2 by 4 for the last stud, extending it through the floor, and attaching it to a joist or other framing underneath. This is particularly effective for walls that are subject to heavy traffic or that support extensive tiling.

### Framing Details for Floor, Walls, and Ceiling

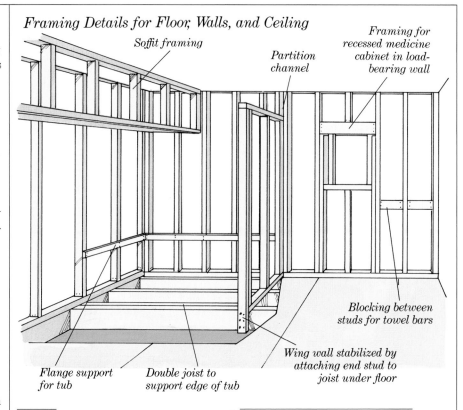

Soffit framing

Partition channel

Framing for recessed medicine cabinet in load-bearing wall

Blocking between studs for towel bars

Wing wall stabilized by attaching end stud to joist under floor

Flange support for tub

Double joist to support edge of tub

### Soffits

A soffit is a boxlike structure that creates a lower ceiling over certain features, such as a vanity or a bathtub, or fills in the space between the top of the wall cabinets and the ceiling. It is constructed on a simple ladder frame covered with plasterboard. Build the soffit after you have applied the wallboard to the main walls and the ceiling—or before if you are installing lights and wiring in the soffit.

Frame the soffit with 2 by 2s to make it easier to drive nails or screws in both directions. Choose perfectly straight lumber—any warps or bows will show clearly. You can also use 2 by 3s or 2 by 4s, which require toenailing but are more stable.

The easiest method of construction is to build an L-shaped ladder frame on the floor and then secure it in place overhead by nailing or screwing one rail into the ceiling joists and the other into the wall studs.

### Recessed Medicine Cabinets

Most medicine cabinets are designed to fit within a standard stud space, which is 14½ inches wide. If the cabinet is wider than that, or if its location does not align with the studs, you will have to frame an opening for it. If you are cutting only one stud, you should be able to use a single 2 by 4 for the header and the sill. Cut and fit vertical 2 by 4s for the sides of the opening, spacing them so that the cabinet will just fit between them.

### Blocking

Installing special blocking within the bathroom wall will later act as supports for accessories. Nail 2 by 6 or larger blocks between the studs where the towel bars, grab bars, and so forth will be installed. Typical heights above the floor are 72 to 84 inches for the top of a wall cabinet, 36 to 48 inches for a towel bar, and waist height for grab bars. Nail 2 by 4 blocks between the studs just above the rim of the bathtub to which the wall backing can be attached.

### Windows

When framing a window over a countertop, you must first determine the height of the finished sill. Will you place it flush with the countertop or above the back splash? If the finished windowsill will be flush with the countertop, be sure to take into account the thickness of the finish floor and of the countertop (if these have not yet been installed) as well as the thickness of the finished sill, and allow extra clearance for shimming when you lay out the height of the rough sill.

### Skylights

A bathroom skylight is framed in the same way as any other skylight. However, you will have less maneuvering room when you lay it out because the ceiling area is small and because the fixtures and any built-in cabinets will create strong axis lines. Normally you have some leeway in locating a skylight so that it can be positioned between rafters, but in a bathroom you may have to cut through more rafters or ceiling joists than you had anticipated just so that you can align the skylight with the other features of the room.

### Pocket Doors

Pocket doors are available in kits, which include a frame that is recessed into the wall. When planning the header, allow for the frame as well as for the door opening. There should be no plumbing, wiring, or other obstructions inside the wall where the frame goes.

### Bathtubs

A bathtub built into an alcove or a corner is installed against the framing, not against the finish wall, so the framed opening should be just large enough for the tub to slide into place against the studs. Adjust the stud spacings where the faucet will be installed so that a stud will not get in the way of the plumbing.

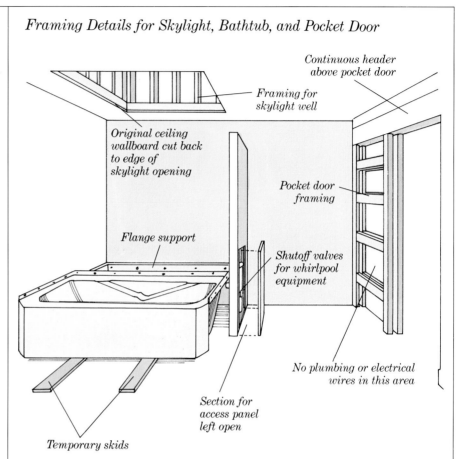

*Framing Details for Skylight, Bathtub, and Pocket Door*

*Continuous header above pocket door*

*Framing for skylight well*

*Original ceiling wallboard cut back to edge of skylight opening*

*Pocket door framing*

*Flange support*

*Shutoff valves for whirlpool equipment*

*Section for access panel left open*

*No plumbing or electrical wires in this area*

*Temporary skids*

### Shower Stalls

If you are using a prefabricated shower pan or stall, frame the walls so that it will fit snugly against the studs. (See page 94 for more information on building shower stalls.)

## Plumbing

The bathroom represents the major part of a residential plumbing system, so changing the plumbing can be complicated. The basic fixtures for most bathrooms are a toilet, a bathtub, a shower, and a washbasin, but your bathroom may also have a second washbasin, a bidet, or a steam room. Even if you do not plan to move any of the fixtures, you should review the guidelines in this section

to make sure that the plumbing is adequate. The drainpipes and vent pipes should be considered first.

### Drainpipes and Vent Pipes

The main considerations for drain- and vent pipes are size, slope, and venting requirements; rough-in dimensions; and use of proper fittings. A bathroom requires a branch drain, at least 3 inches in diameter, connected to the main drain of the house. Your present branch drain probably meets these specifications. Drainpipe sizes are actually determined by the number of fixture units, not by the type of fixture, but the typical required sizes are as follows: toilet, 3 inches, inside diameter;

shower, 2 inches; bathtub (with or without a shower), 1½ inches; bidet, 1½ inches; and washbasin, 1¼ inches. In practice 1½-inch drainpipes are commonly used for washbasins. If two washbasins share the same drainpipe, it should be 2 inches inside diameter, although 1½-inch pipe may be allowed for the first vertical section. Check the local building code.

If you are extending a drain, you must consider the slope. Drainpipes must slope ¼ inch per foot, so if the existing drain is strapped close to the bottom of the floor joists there may not be enough clearance to extend it upstream to a new fixture, unless the new pipe runs parallel to the joists and can be suspended between them. Failing this, it may be possible to bore through the joists for a 1½-inch or 2-inch drainpipe, provided the joists are 2 by 10s or 2 by 12s and the holes are at least 2 inches from the edge. Otherwise it will be necessary to hang the new drainpipe below the joists and connect it to the main drain farther downstream in order to get the proper flow. It is not necessary to vent all the fixtures into the same branch drain. It may be more convenient to connect a new fixture to a different drain, as long as it is large enough.

All plumbing fixtures must be vented above the roof. If you are not moving a fixture very far, you can probably use the original vent. A drainpipe must be vented within a certain distance of the fixture trap (this is called the maximum trap arm distance) and before it changes from the horizontal to the vertical. An exception is often made for the toilet drainpipe, which can be vented after it changes to the vertical. Codes prohibit changing the direction of the vent pipe from vertical to horizontal at any point lower than 6 inches above the flood rim of the fixture. This is typically a minimum of 36 inches above the floor for a washbasin, 21 inches for a toilet, and 20 to 26 inches for a bathtub. If a window

## Rough Plumbing for a Bathroom

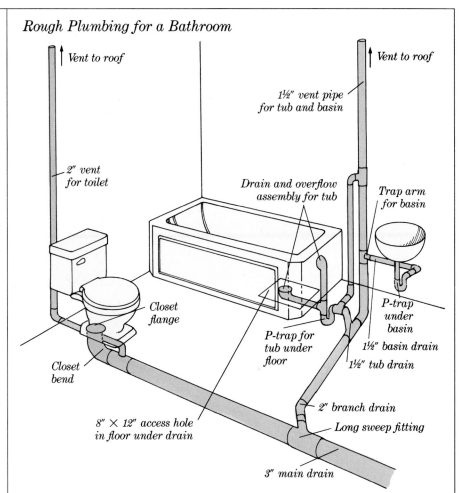

*Vent to roof*

*Vent to roof*

*1½" vent pipe for tub and basin*

*2" vent for toilet*

*Drain and overflow assembly for tub*

*Trap arm for basin*

*Closet flange*

*P-trap for tub under floor*

*P-trap under basin*

*1½" basin drain*

*1½" tub drain*

*Closet bend*

*2" branch drain*

*Long sweep fitting*

*8" × 12" access hole in floor under drain*

*3" main drain*

or other obstruction makes it necessary to change the direction of the vent pipe before this point, you have two choices. One is to offset the vent pipe with two 45-degree fittings to clear the obstruction. The other is to run the vertical vent pipe along one side of the window and run a horizontal trap arm from the fixture to the pipe (as long as it does not exceed the maximum trap arm distance). If you are venting a washbasin in an island, where a vertical vent pipe cannot be concealed in a wall, you can use a special loop arrangement. Check the local code for maximum trap arm distance (typically 3 feet for a 1½-inch drainpipe and up to 5 feet for a 2-inch pipe) and for other venting requirements.

Obtain rough-in dimensions for each new fixture that you plan to install. You can get them from the supplier or the manufacturer. If you are replacing an old toilet with a new one, check the location of the floor flange. The rough-in dimension for most new toilets is 12 inches from the center of the flange to the surface of the finish wall behind it. Many older toilets were centered 10 inches or 14 inches from the finish wall. If this was the case with your old toilet, the new toilet may not fit, or it may be too far from the wall. If you are installing a wall-mounted toilet, you must install a separate carrier in the wall as part of the rough plumbing.

When roughing in drainpipes, maintain the proper slope and use the proper fitting for each connection

## Plumbing Details for Bathroom Fixtures

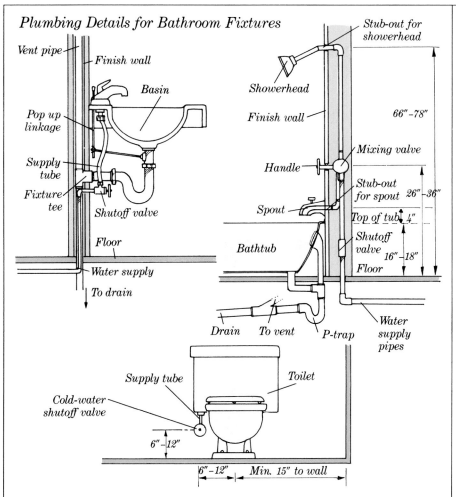

Vent pipe

Finish wall

Basin

Pop up linkage

Supply tube

Fixture tee

Shutoff valve

Floor

Water supply

To drain

Stub-out for showerhead

Showerhead

Finish wall

66"–78"

Mixing valve

Handle

Stub-out for spout 26"–36"

Spout

Top of tub 4"

Shutoff valve 16"–18"

Bathtub

Floor

Drain  To vent  P-trap

Water supply pipes

Supply tube  Toilet

Cold-water shutoff valve

6"–12"

6"–12"  Min. 15" to wall

and each change in direction. For instance, the tee fitting for a washbasin must be a fixture tee, not a sanitary tee, which looks almost identical. For double basins you can run the trap arms into a double fixture tee, which has a 2-inch outlet on the bottom, a 1½-inch outlet at the top, and a 1½-inch inlet on each side for the trap arms. If you are unsure about the proper fittings to use, refer to a plumbing manual or consult a qualified plumber.

Install the bathtub as part of the rough plumbing so that you can fill it with water and test it before you close in any of the pipes. It is easiest to attach the trip-lever drain and overflow assembly first. Then slide

the tub into position, being very careful not to scratch or mar the surface. Avoid wearing watches, rings, and belt buckles that may rub against the tub while you are jostling it into place. A cast-iron tub will stay in place, but steel or fiberglass tubs must be supported at the rim with ledger boards, and the flanges must be secured against the framing with galvanized nails or screws.

If you are moving the toilet, you will need to rough in a new floor flange. The top of the flange should be flush with the surface of the finish floor. If you will be adding underlayment to the existing floor after the flange is in place, cut an 8-inch square piece of the underlayment or of some similar material, with a hole in it for the flange outlet, to put under the flange before you install it.

## Water Supply Pipes

Run the water pipes after the drain- and vent pipes are installed. Copper and PVC plastic supply pipes are the most popular choice, although not all local codes allow the use of plastic. Galvanized pipes, which must be cut and threaded, are another alternative, and a new, flexible plastic pipe called polybutylene (PB) is allowed in some areas. The size of the pipes is determined by the number of fixture units being served, the water pressure, and the length of the runs, but as a rule of thumb use ½-inch pipe for all hot-water lines and for cold-water lines that serve one fixture. Use ¾-inch pipe for cold-water lines that serve more than one fixture.

If you are connecting new copper pipes to old galvanized pipes, use a special dielectric union or intermediate brass fitting. This will help to prevent the corrosion caused by joining dissimilar metals.

Typical rough-in dimensions for water supply stubs are 19 inches above the floor for a washbasin, 8 inches for a toilet, 26 inches for a bathtub, and 46 inches for a shower, but you can adjust these dimensions to fit the manufacturer's specifications or your own needs. Double sinks should have separate stub-outs and shutoff valves.

You may want to add a second water heater to serve the new bathroom. It will increase the capacity of the system, and the shorter runs will give you hot water faster. An electric heater can be located almost anywhere; some of them are small enough to fit inside a vanity. A gas heater must have a flue and an adequate source of fresh combustion air, and certain bathroom, bedroom, and closet installations are prohibited. Check with the local building inspection department to learn the specific requirements in your area.

## Wiring

The rough wiring for most bathrooms involves installing outlets for new light fixtures, adding or moving switches, adding or moving receptacles, protecting receptacles with ground fault circuit interrupter (GFCI) devices, and adding new circuits for specific fixtures. The techniques and code requirements are similar to those for other rooms, except that the presence of water and grounded pipes makes safety an even more important issue. Be sure to observe the local code, especially in the following situations.

□ A separate circuit is required for each permanently installed fixture above a certain amperage—for example, a whirlpool bathtub, an electric wall heater, or an electric water heater. Radiant-heat lamps and ceiling fans may also require separate circuits, depending on the local building code.

□ All outlets and any motors for bathtub equipment must be protected by a GFCI device that automatically deadens the outlet the moment any unusual condition creates the potential for electric shock. These devices are available as circuit breakers that are installed in the main breaker panel and protect an entire circuit, or as receptacles. A GFCI receptacle can be wired so that it protects other receptacles as well. It is best to install one that protects all the other receptacles in the bathroom only. This eliminates excessive nuisance tripping. It also renders the device accessible, so that it can be easily reset. Bathroom outlets do not usually require a separate circuit of their own. However, it may be necessary to run a new circuit if the existing house circuits are not grounded, or if they are loaded to capacity.

□ Bathroom lights should be on a separate lighting circuit. They should not be on the same circuit as receptacles or individual fixtures.

### Rough Wiring for a Bathroom

To power source

Fan housing mounted in ceiling

Minimum horizontal distance between tub and outlet typically 5' unless outlet is GFCI

Recessed light fixtures mounted in soffit

To power source

Switch loop for fan

Switch loop for lights

Minimum vertical distance between tub rim and electrical fixture typically 8'

Copper water pipes

Switch

To power source

Access panel opening

Outlets with GFCI protection

Spa-style tub

Separate ground wire from system ground, motor frame, and all metal pipes

New designated circuit for whirlpool motor to power source

To power source

□ For reasons of safety, no fixtures, switches, or outlets can be located within a certain distance of a bathtub. The minimum is usually 5 feet horizontally and 7½ feet vertically, but check the local code. You may be able to install lights or switches within the restricted area if you protect them with GFCI devices, air switches, or low-voltage switch relays.

### New Circuits

As you plan new circuits, ask yourself whether the present electrical system can meet the new demand. There are two things to consider. One is the available space for new circuit breakers, including a double space for each 240-volt breaker. The other is the electrical capacity of the main service entrance. If the present panel has few or no empty spaces for new

breakers, you can use either half-size wafer breakers to get more space or install a subpanel (typically 60 amperes) for any new circuits. Check with the local building department to determine where the subpanel may be installed. Closets or other restricted spaces may not be allowed.

Most homes have enough electrical capacity to meet the added demands of a new bathroom, provided that you are not adding any major appliances, such as a water heater. The present service must be properly grounded, however, and it must be at least 100 amperes. If you are in any doubt, have a load calculation done by an electrical contractor to make certain that the new demand won't overload the system. If it will, you will have to upgrade the service entrance.

## Installing Heating and Venting Units

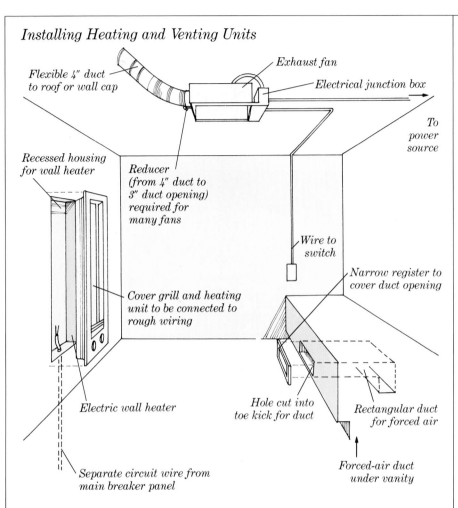

Flexible 4" duct to roof or wall cap

Exhaust fan

Electrical junction box

To power source

Recessed housing for wall heater

Reducer (from 4" duct to 3" duct opening) required for many fans

Wire to switch

Narrow register to cover duct opening

Cover grill and heating unit to be connected to rough wiring

Electric wall heater

Hole cut into toe kick for duct

Rectangular duct for forced air

Forced-air duct under vanity

Separate circuit wire from main breaker panel

## Electrical Boxes

Locate boxes for lights, switches, and outlets according to the design plan. Avoid locating boxes for receptacles where they might interfere with a mirror, a medicine cabinet, a towel bar, or a complicated back splash. If the box must be installed in the side of the vanity, you must use flexible armored cable where the wiring is exposed inside the cabinet.

Note: Most boxes extend ½ inch out from the studs to accommodate the thickness of standard wallboard. However, some outlets may be located within the back splash area. Be sure to extend the box far enough out to accommodate both the wallboard and the back splash material. The face of the box must be flush with the finished surface.

## Electrical Cable

For most installations the codes will allow the use of Romex nonmetallic sheathed cable. Use No. 12 for 20-ampere circuits and No. 10 or larger for 240-volt circuits. Observe the same rules for running cable in a bathroom as in any other room. Staple it every 4½ feet and within 8 inches of plastic boxes and 12 inches of metal boxes. Many areas do not allow wiring to be run horizontally through exterior wall studs; it must be run under the floor and brought up through the soleplate for each outlet. Check the local code.

## Heating and Ventilation

There are several ways to add a heating system to the bathroom. You can extend an existing forced-air system, extend an existing hot-water (hydronic) system, or install a new electric baseboard or wall heater. Because wall space in bathrooms is limited, you may have difficulty finding a good location for a forced-air register. The usual solution is to locate it under the toe kick of the vanity cabinet by bringing a duct up through the floor or out from the back wall. Run a transition elbow or a straight rectangular duct on the floor where the vanity will go; cut a hole in the front of the toe kick for it; and set the vanity in place. Cover the hole with a 3¼-inch by 10-inch grill.

Electric wall heaters are wired with either a 120-volt or a 240-volt circuit. The 240-volt circuit requires three-wire cable and a double circuit breaker. The cost is offset by the more efficient use of electricity.

An exhaust fan is desirable in any bathroom, and it is required in bathrooms that have no windows that can be opened. All fans should be ducted to the outside through the roof or a nearby wall. To install a fan, set the housing in place between two ceiling joists. Install a termination cap in the wall or in the roof by cutting a hole approximately 4½ inches in diameter through the sheathing and attaching the cap from the outside. Run 4-inch flexible duct from the fan housing to the termination cap, using a tightening band or sheet-metal screws to secure it at each end.

Run a two-wire No. 12 feeder cable from the circuit breaker panel to the fan junction box. Then run cable from the fan to a switch box on the wall. Use one two-wire, one three-wire, or two two-wire cables (all with ground wires), depending on how many switches are needed to control the fan motor, the radiant-heat lamp, the light, and so on. All of the wires in this switch loop will be hot, so mark any white wires with black tape.

## Preparing Walls and Ceilings

The walls and ceiling of a bathroom are covered in the usual way. They are also insulated in the usual way, except that it is advisable to staple polyethylene sheeting over the insulation before you apply the wallboard to protect it against damage from water vapor. Use a utility knife to cut out the sheeting around windows, electrical boxes, and so forth.

Wallboard is likewise installed in the usual way, although you may have to make numerous cutouts for plumbing, wiring, and mechanical devices. Special moisture resistant wallboard is available for areas that are likely to get wet. Use it around the washbasin, in the upper wall area of a shower stall or bathtub enclosure, or as a backing in areas where tile will be installed over a mortar bed. Use mesh tape and waterproof joint compound to cover the joints. Do not apply moisture resistant wallboard to the ceiling; it is heavy and will sag over time. Do not use it as a tub or shower backing in areas where the tile will not be set in a mortar bed—special nonorganic tile-backing units work better. If you are patching new wallboard into old wallboard or plaster, cut the old material back to a corner, a door, a window, or some other feature in order to make the joint less obvious.

There are several methods for patching holes in old wallboard. Small holes can be filled with patching compound; you may want to cover them first with adhesive-backed fiberglass mesh tape. Trim larger holes to a regular shape, such as a triangle. Cut a patch of wallboard to fit exactly into the hole and a wide strip of plywood or wallboard to serve as backing. Slip the backing strip inside the wall behind the hole and secure it with wallboard screws or paneling adhesive. Glue or screw the patch to the backing and tape the seams. Very large holes can be patched by cutting the wallboard

back to the nearest studs and fitting in a new piece.

The baseboard and the other trim can be installed at this point, except where it abuts built-in fixtures.

Any surfaces that will be painted, whether they are old or new, must be clean, dry, and free of peeling paint. Use abrasive paper or TSP to roughen glossy surfaces so that the new paint will stick. Final painting can be done before or after the fixtures and cabinets are installed, although it is easier to do beforehand. Do the ceiling first, at least, to avoid spattering paint on the new fixtures and cabinets.

Wallpaper and similar coverings are usually applied last, but you may want to apply them before you install the fixtures and the cabinets if you can be sure that they won't be soiled

or damaged during the final stages of construction. Prepare the wall surfaces as if you were preparing them for painting. Some wallpapers will not adhere to an unsized wall. Others will, so follow the dealer's recommendations as regards sizing.

Information on finishing walls begins on page 103.

Information on finishing walls begins on page 103.

**Opposite:** *A banjo-style countertop extends over the toilet top, providing a smooth line and extra shelf space in a small powder room. Because powder rooms are small, they provide an excellent opportunity to use slightly more expensive finish materials. Display art in a powder room, so that guests can enjoy it while they freshen up.*

### Preparing a Bathtub Surround

Moisture-resistant wallboard

Wallboard corner

Joints sealed with fiberglass mesh tape or waterproofing compound

Standard wallboard applied horizontally

Nailheads coated with waterproofing compound or sealer

Tile-backing units

*Repair technique*

Patching mesh

Spackling compound or plaster

*Tub alcove requires waterproof materials and careful preparation*

# INSTALLING FIXTURES

W hen it comes to installing fixtures, preparation is often nine-tenths of the job. The following guidelines explain how to install each bathroom fixture from start to finish. You will not usually do all the work on a given fixture at once. Rather, you will do certain parts of the work for all of the fixtures at the same time. Examples include framing, rough plumbing, installing wallboard and tile, and finish plumbing.

## Shower Stalls

You have three options for a new shower stall. You can choose a prefabricated, one-piece unit; a custom-built stall with a prefabricated shower pan; or a custom-built stall with a custom-built shower pan. A prefabricated unit is the easiest to install. You can build a shower stall with a prefabricated base if you have basic carpentry, plumbing, and ceramic tile-setting skills.

### Prefabricated Units

You can buy plastic or fiberglass units that include everything except the plumbing. These showers can be installed by one person in less than a day. The most difficult part may be getting the unit into the bathroom because most are too large to pass through a standard doorway. Some units have a ceiling; others don't.
1. Build conventional framed walls to support the unit. Space the studs evenly and adjust the spacing where the plumbing will go so that the studs

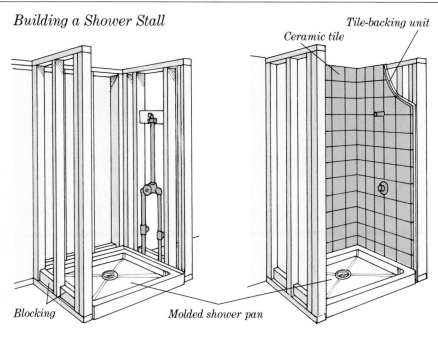

**Building a Shower Stall**

Blocking — Molded shower pan

Tile-backing unit — Ceramic tile

will not interfere with the faucet. The width of the enclosure must be exact, so check the manufacturer's specifications or measure the unit itself at the base. Note: Some local codes may require you to install fireproof wallboard in the opening before you install the shower. This provision applies particularly to buildings with multiple dwelling units.
2. Rough in a 2-inch P-trap under the floor and stub up the 2-inch drainpipe out of the floor where the drain hole will go. Cut it off at the height specified by the manufacturer's instructions. Rough in the faucet and the showerhead and cut holes in the walls of the stall to fit the showerhead stub and the faucet stems.
3. Install the drain fitting in the floor of the shower unit, using plumber's putty around the flange. Remove the gasket and the retaining ring.
4. Lift the shower unit into place, centering the drain fitting down over the drain stub. Some manufacturers recommend setting the unit on a ½-inch bed of mortar or quick-setting plaster compound to provide maximum support. Nail the top and side flanges to the studs with galvanized

roofing nails. Secure the drain fitting by slipping the gasket down around the 2-inch drainpipe and screwing the retaining ring down on it to compress it.
5. Finish plumbing the faucet and the showerhead: Apply caulk around cutouts and attach the fittings and escutcheons to the rough plumbing. Test the plumbing.
6. Apply wallboard or other wallcovering to the framing, bringing it over the wall flanges of the shower unit. Finish the wallcovering to match the surrounding areas—with paint, wallpaper, tile, or other materials.

### Custom-Built Stalls

You will need to have the dimensions of the shower pan or the pan itself on hand before you frame the walls. Before you begin construction, decide what special features you want. For instance, shower faucet handles are normally set 42 to 48 inches, and showerheads 66 to 78 inches, above the floor. However, you may want to set the handles at a different height, or set several showerheads, activated individually, at different heights to accommodate different users. You can also plan to have grab bars, a seat, or recessed shelves or alcoves.

1. Construct the sidewall that will take the plumbing. Set it at a right angle to the back wall. Space the studs so that they will not interfere with the plumbing, and nail blocking between the studs where the top edge of the shower pan will go.

2. Rough in a 2-inch P-trap under the floor, with a vertical drain stub that comes up through the floor where the drain hole will go. Rough in the water supply pipes, the shower valve, and the elbow for the showerhead. If possible, provide shutoff valves that can be reached from an access door on the back of the plumbing wall.

3. Install the drain fitting in the shower pan and remove the retaining ring and gasket from the fitting. Spread a ½-inch layer of quick-setting plaster compound on the floor. Set the pan in place and level it. Slip the gasket down around the 2-inch drainpipe and screw the retaining ring down on it to compress it. Test the plumbing for leaks.

4. Finish the framing around the shower pan. At the top of the pan, insert blocking between the studs. Secure the nailing flanges to the studs and blocking with galvanized roofing nails.

5. Line the inside of the stall with tile-backing units up to the point where the tile will end. Most brands of backing come in 3-foot by 5-foot panels, but some manufacturers also offer 4-foot by 5-foot and 4-foot by 8-foot panels. Nail them to the studs with galvanized roofing nails, lapping the backing over the flange of the shower pan. Leave a ¼-inch gap around the bottom of the panels. Seal the joints with fiberglass mesh tape and waterproof joint compound or tile adhesive. Cover the upper portion of the stall and the outside of the walls with wallboard.

6. Finish the inside of the stall with tile, marble, or other appropriate surface material. Finish the outside to match the surrounding walls. Install the finish plumbing and a glass shower door according to the manufacturer's instructions (see page 109). If you have to drill holes into the tile to secure the doorframe, use a special carbide-tipped bit. If possible, align the holes with the grout lines to make drilling easier.

## Bathtubs

Install bathtubs as part of the rough plumbing, before the walls are closed in and before the floor is finished. The tub is the hardest of all bathroom fixtures to install, for the same reasons that it is the hardest to remove: It is big, cumbersome, and heavy, and the plumbing connections are usually made inside a tight space. To install even a lightweight fiberglass tub you will need at least one helper; if the bathtub is made of cast iron, you will probably need several.

For purposes of installation, there are two types of bathtub. Tubs with one finished side are designed to be installed in an alcove. Tubs with no finished sides are designed to be completely surrounded by a built-in platform. Differences in size, material, and configuration can pose special problems, however, so be sure to get installation instructions from the dealer or the manufacturer.

### Built-In Tubs

The following guidelines explain how to install a standard enameled steel tub 30 inches wide by 60 inches long. They should give you a general sense of how to install any bathtub into an alcove.

1. Frame the walls so that the opening is just large enough to enable you to slide the tub into place against the studs. The end studs should be recessed slightly so that the finish surface of the wallcovering will be flush with the finished side of the tub. Adjust the stud spacings so that the studs will not interfere with the installation of the faucet.

2. Slide the tub into place, level it with shims under the bottom, and mark where the bottom of the rim touches the studs. Pull the tub out again and nail 2 by 4 ledgers to the studs just under the marks. These ledgers will support the rim of the tub. Mark, measure, and nail carefully. The ledger boards must be just the right height off the floor to enable the rim to make full contact. Slide the tub in again and double-check all of your measurements. If the P-trap has not yet been roughed in, mark on the floor the exact center of the drain hole. Slide the tub back out.

3. If the P-trap and the drainpipe have not been roughed in, cut an access hole in the floor approximately 4 to 6 inches wide that extends 12 inches out from the center of the end wall. Rough in a 1½-inch P-trap below floor level, with the slip nut fitting centered directly under the overflow pipe of the tub.

4. You can rough in the water supply pipes, the mixing valve, and the stubs for the spout and showerhead now or after the tub is installed, depending on how easy it will be to get behind the tub later. The spout is usually installed 4 inches above the tub rim, the faucets 4 to 6 inches above the spout, and the showerhead 66 to 78 inches above the floor, but you can adjust these heights to suit your needs. You can even place the faucets on one wall and the showerhead or the spout on another, if you wish. Install shutoff valves for both hot and cold water.

5. Connect the drain elbow to the tub, applying a ring of plumber's putty under the flange. Tighten it by holding the drain-tee steady with the handle of a pair of pliers or with a similar forked tool while you tighten the nut underneath. You can attach the overflow pipe and the tailpiece now or when the tub is in place. Cut the tailpiece so that it will fit 1 to 1½ inches down into the P-trap.

6. If the tub is not insulated, fit pieces of fiberglass blanket insulation around it. If there is room, put some under the tub as well. Do not compress the insulation.

## Installing a Platform Tub

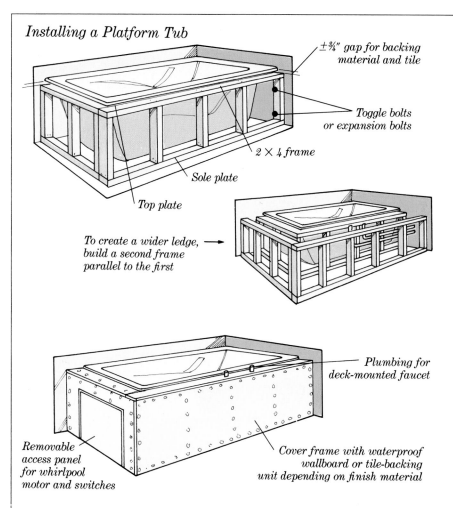

±¾" gap for backing material and tile

Toggle bolts or expansion bolts

2 × 4 frame

Sole plate

Top plate

To create a wider ledge, build a second frame parallel to the first

Plumbing for deck-mounted faucet

Removable access panel for whirlpool motor and switches

Cover frame with waterproof wallboard or tile-backing unit depending on finish material

7. Slide the tub into place. Use shims where necessary to make it stable and level. Drive 7d or 8d galvanized box nails above the steel flange and into the studs so that the nail heads hold the flange to the walls. If the tub is made of fiberglass, drill pilot holes into the flange before you nail through it. A cast-iron tub need not be secured to the walls.

8. Connect the drain. The tailpiece below the drain tee should slide into the P-trap below the floor. Tighten the slip joints on the P-trap and the drain tee securely. Install the stopper mechanism according to the manufacturer's instructions. To test for leaks, and later for the plumbing inspection, fill the tub with water and let it sit for a few hours. Then open the stopper and let the water run down the drain.

9. Apply tile-backing units or moisture resistant wallboard (depending on the finish material) to the framing around the tub. Lap it over the tub flange but leave a ¼-inch gap around the top of the rim. This gap should be caulked when the tile or other finish material is installed. Seal the joints with fiberglass mesh tape and moisture resistant joint compound or tile adhesive.

10. If you install tile, use a level to mark guidelines for the first (bottom) row. Not all tub rims are level, so don't use the tub rim as a guide.

## Platform Tubs

Most luxury tubs, whether they are whirlpool units or conventional models, are designed for platform installation. Some come with an optional

matching skirt to finish the side, but most units are finished with custom materials applied over a frame that is built on-site. The guidelines presented here are applicable to most installations, but you may need to modify them to accommodate a particular type of tub, choice of finish, or detail in the plumbing. For instance, if the tub is light enough to allow two or three people to lift it into place, you can build the platform first and then lower the tub into it. You may have to exercise ingenuity in doing some of the finish work before the rough plumbing so that the rim of the tub will rest on a finished surface. If you want the rim to be covered or to be flush with the surrounding surface, you can finish the top of the platform deck at the same time as you finish the sides. In some cases there may not be enough room to install a platform all the way around the tub, so the finish walls will come down to the rim on one or more sides as they do on a built-in tub. This eliminates the need to set some of the rim on a finished surface, but it requires a waterproof joint to prevent water spilled onto the rim from backing up behind the wall. Tubs made of acrylic and other plastic materials can expand and contract with changes in temperature; they must have strong support around the rim.

1. It is usually easier to install the tub first and then build the supporting framework in place so that it fits properly and so that you can leave just the right amount of clearance under the rim of the tub to install the finish material. This is the only option if the tub is made of cast iron. Be sure that the drain line and the P-trap are roughed in below the floor and that there is an access hole through the floor for connecting the tub drain to the P-trap.

2. Build the frame out of 2 by 4s, spacing the studs 16 inches apart. Attach the framing to the walls and floor with construction screws or with nails and construction glue. Use toggle bolts or expansion bolts at the wall if the frame does not abut a stud.

If you want a wider ledge, use 2 by 6 lumber or build another 2 by 4 frame outside the first one. Build a third frame if you want the platform to be more than 16 inches wide. You can rough in the water supply pipes now or in Step 4.

3. Raise the tub about 1 inch, using pry bars, and support it temporarily on blocks. Apply moisture resistant backing material to the top of the framing and seal the joints with mesh tape. Install the tile or other finish material along the top of the ledge where it will be covered by the rim of the tub. Plan the layout carefully to allow for an overhang or nosing around the outside edge. If you plan to install a deck-mounted faucet or spout, remember to allow for the holes. After the adhesives have set up thoroughly, spread a ½-inch layer of mortar or quick-setting plaster on the floor and lower the tub onto it. For a watertight seal, apply a bead of caulk around the bottom of the rim before you lower the tub.

4. Hook up the drain in the same way as you would for a built-in tub. Some drains are located along the side of the tub and others at one end.

5. Rough in the water supply pipes and install the mixing valve and the spout. If there is an integral filler spout below the rim of the tub, you will have to install a vacuum breaker between this spout and the mixing valve. Because the vacuum breaker must be mounted at least 6 inches above the rim of the tub, you will have to run the water line from the mixing valve back to the nearest wall, up the wall to the vacuum breaker, and back to the spout. The vacuum breaker must be accessible for servicing, so install a removable panel or door on one side of the wall.

6. If the tub has a whirlpool unit, it will probably come with the motor and the circulating pipes already installed. The feed wires for the motor should be connected to a separate 120-volt or 240-volt circuit, the voltage depending on the motor. Most local codes require that all metal

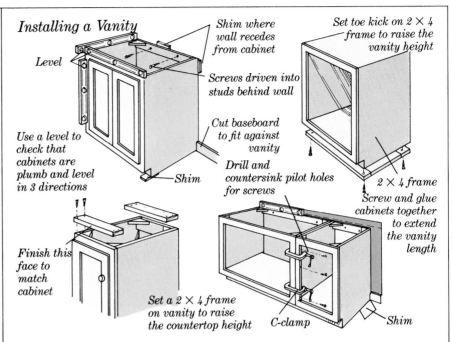

**Installing a Vanity**

Level

Shim where wall recedes from cabinet

Screws driven into studs behind wall

Use a level to check that cabinets are plumb and level in 3 directions

Shim

Cut baseboard to fit against vanity

Drill and countersink pilot holes for screws

Set toe kick on 2 × 4 frame to raise the vanity height

2 × 4 frame

Screw and glue cabinets together to extend the vanity length

Finish this face to match cabinet

Set a 2 × 4 frame on vanity to raise the countertop height

C-clamp

Shim

pipes be bonded to the motor with a separate No. 6 copper ground wire. Some codes also require that the ground wire between the motor and the house grounding system be continuous, and that it be separate from the electrical conduit or cable. The switch that activates the motor must have an approved safety protection device, such as a GFCI. Some units have a push-button air switch on the rim of the tub that activates an electrical switch mounted on the motor.

7. Test the plumbing for leaks by filling the tub. Do not test a whirlpool until there is enough water in the tub to cover all the jets.

8. After the plumbing has been inspected, insulate the tub (see page 95, step 6) and cover the framing with a backing appropriate to the finish material. The latter may be tile, dimensioned-stone, solid surface material, or wood. If the tub has a whirlpool, install a removable panel to provide access to the motor.

## Vanity Cabinets

It is relatively easy to install a vanity. It is also easy to individualize one to meet your special needs. If you want a large vanity, you can combine two or more modular units, or you can have a cabinet custom-made. The standard height for a vanity, including the countertop, is 30 to 32 inches, but you can make it higher, as explained in Step 3.

1. Vanity cabinets are generally open in back to accommodate the plumbing. If yours is not, you can cut out a section of the back to make an opening for the water supply stubs and the drain stubs. You can install the shutoff valves after the vanity is in place, just before you install the countertop, but it is easier to install them beforehand.

2. Be sure that the floor is level. If it is not, put shims under the cabinet or trim down the base to level it. The walls surrounding the cabinet should be flat, without any bumps or bulges.

3. If you wish to make the vanity or the countertop higher, there are four ways to do it. You can use a modular kitchen base cabinet, which is 34½ inches high and 24 inches deep. You can build a base out of 2 by 4s and set the vanity on top of it. You can raise the toe kick by turning the cabinet upside down and screwing wood cleats to the bottom. Finally, you can elevate the countertop by screwing wood cleats to the top of the

vanity and attaching the countertop to them. Finish the faces of the cleats to match the vanity.

4. Measure the height of the cabinet. Using a level, draw a line on the wall at that height. If the vanity is in a corner, draw lines on both walls. Drill pilot holes into the hanging cleat on the cabinet. Make sure that each hole is centered over a stud. Attach the hanging cleat to the wall with 2½-inch screws. Be sure that the weight of the cabinet rests on the floor, not on the screws. Shim behind the screws if there is a gap between the floor and the front of the cabinet.

5. If you are combining two or more units, fasten them together with C-clamps. Drill pilot holes into the side of the stile of one cabinet and drive screws through these holes into the stile of the adjacent unit. Make sure that the cabinets are level and that the face frames are tight and flush. Tightening the screws will often pull a unit out of line. If this happens, add shims or remove them.

## Countertops

There is a different installation technique for each type of countertop, but all of these techniques are similar in certain respects. In taking measurements, allow for a 1-inch overhang in front of the vanity. Allow for a ½-inch overhang on any side that does not abut a wall. There should be a back splash and, if necessary, side splashes to prevent water from marring the walls and seeping down behind the cabinet. The back splash is usually 4 inches high.

The easiest countertop to install is one made of cast polymer or solid surface material with a washbasin molded into it. All you have to do is run a bead of silicone caulk around the top edge of the cabinet and set the countertop into place. It is usually easiest to install the faucet and drain fitting beforehand. To install any other type of countertop, you must cut out a hole for the sink and add a back splash. With some materials you

can build and install the countertop yourself; with others you can do the installation, but you should hire a professional to measure and fabricate the countertop.

### Ceramic Tile

Tile is an excellent material for countertops and back splashes because it is attractive, durable, and easy to clean. Installing a tile countertop is a simple do-it-yourself project using the thinsetting technique described here.

Plan the trim and the accent pieces early and order them along with the tile. If the tile will be trimmed with a wood edge, the wood should be installed, stained, and sealed before you set the tile.

1. Prepare the substrate. An acceptable installation for a bathroom counter is ½-inch tile-backing units nailed to a ¾-inch plywood base. Tile can also be laid directly over plywood, but the plywood must be carefully sealed with an epoxy-based mastic; latex or epoxy modifiers must be added to the grout mix; and the grout must be sealed after it sets.

Start by installing a ¾-inch plywood base over the vanity. If you are not adding a mortar float or tile-backing units to the top, raise the plywood by attaching 1 by 3 strips to the bottom along the edges. This provides a backing for the tiles along the front edge and keeps them from interfering with the drawers. Screw the top in from below to make future removal easier. Check to make sure that it is level. If it is not, level it by inserting shims between the vanity and the plywood.

Cut out the basin hole (see page 101). If you are installing a recessed basin, set it in place now. Use the method described for slab countertops if the tile will be flush with the top of the basin rim. If you plan to surround the basin with quarter round trim, you can clamp the basin to the bottom of the base with

special mounting clips that screw into the plywood. Surface-mounted basins are installed after the tiling is done.

2. Lay out the tile pattern and test it with a dry run, placing all the tiles exactly where you want them. Start with the trim pieces, edging tiles first, and continue with the field tiles. Use tile spacers to maintain uniform grout lines. If possible avoid narrow cuts in the back. All of the trim pieces should be laid out so that the grout lines follow the grout lines of the field tiles.

3. When you are satisfied with the layout for the front and back edges, lay out the tiles around the basin. If the basin will be surface-mounted, mark the tiles for cutting by laying them in place and scribing them from underneath. Cut them with a tile cutter or nippers. The rim of the basin will cover the raw edges.

If the basin is recessed, fit the trim pieces around it. Then cut the tiles where they abut the trim pieces, allowing for the grout line. These cuts must be made smoothly and accurately because the raw edges will remain visible, so it is best to make them as you set the tile.

4. When you have completed the layout, remove the tiles and mark any pieces to be cut. In a large bucket using special mortar-mixing paddles, mix adhesives according to package directions. Thinset adhesives are a combination of liquid and dry materials. Mix only the amount you will be able to use in about 1 hour. Let mixed adhesive rest for about 10 minutes before applying.

Adhesive is applied in two steps: First it is spread, then combed. Use a notched trowel for both steps. Different adhesives have different open times (the time during which the tile may be applied, before the adhesive becomes too dry), so check the instructions on the package. Also note any safety precautions regarding ventilation, open flames, and skin contact.

Start at one of the front corners. Install the bullnose tiles or the trim pieces first. Use spacers to keep the tiles evenly aligned. Place each tile

## Installing Countertops

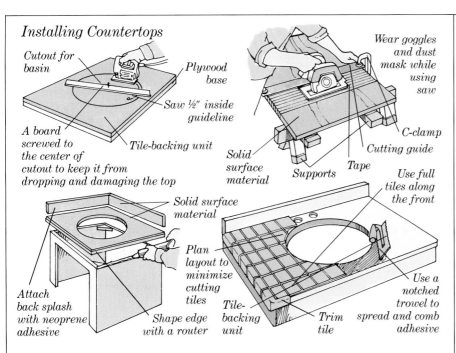

Cutout for basin

A board screwed to the center of cutout to keep it from dropping and damaging the top

Saw ½" inside guideline

Plywood base

Tile-backing unit

Solid surface material

Supports

Tape

C-clamp

Cutting guide

Wear goggles and dust mask while using saw

Use full tiles along the front

Solid surface material

Attach back splash with neoprene adhesive

Shape edge with a router

Plan layout to minimize cutting tiles

Tile-backing unit

Trim tile

Use a notched trowel to spread and comb adhesive

carefully and press it down with a slight twisting motion.

5. Spread adhesive over a small area holding the notched trowel at about a 45-degree angle to achieve maximum coverage. When you have installed all of the trim pieces, install the field tiles. Continue across the surface of the countertop, as before. Use nippers to cut the tiles to fit around obstructions. When you have set the last row of countertop tiles, work your way up the back splash wall. Finish the top edge with bullnose tiles.

When all of the tiles are set, remove the excess mastic as quickly as possible. Then let the work dry for one or two days.

6. Grout the joints, following the instructions provided by the manufacturer. Spread the grout with a rubber float, working it diagonally to the grout lines. Force the grout firmly into the joints, using the handle of a toothbrush or some other small tool. Clean off the excess grout with a damp sponge, wringing it out frequently in clean water. Let the surface residue dry to form a haze. Then polish the tiles with a cheesecloth or other soft cloth. Cover the countertop with plastic sheeting for two or three days to

let the grout cure properly. After two weeks seal the grout to keep it clean and free of mildew.

### Plastic Laminate

High-pressure laminates come in a wide choice of colors and patterns. The laminate itself is only about ¹/₁₆ inch thick; it must be bonded to a stable substrate of particleboard or plywood. You can do this yourself, provided you are familiar with the process. Otherwise buy a length of ready-made postformed countertop or order a custom-made unit from a specialty shop. You can have the fabricator install the countertop, or you can install it yourself using the following techniques.

1. Determine how long the countertop should be. Remember to allow for overhangs and for the thickness of the back splash pieces on the ends. Buy the next longest size. Buy separate end splash pieces and end caps as needed.

2. Cut the countertop to length. Use a framing square to mark the cutting line along the top of the counter and up the back splash. If the corner of the wall is out of square, adjust the cutting line to compensate. Place masking tape over the line and

make a fresh mark on the masking tape. This will protect the edge from chipping when it is cut. Support the countertop well on both sides of the cutting line to prevent it from breaking. Use a sharp handsaw with 10 to 12 points per inch, a reciprocating saw, or a circular saw with a sharp blade. If you use a handsaw, bear lightly on the upstrokes and heavily on the downstrokes. If you use a reciprocating saw, the teeth should point downward. If they do not, transfer the cutting line to the bottom of the countertop and cut from that side. Do the same thing with a circular saw. Smooth the edge of the cut with a file or a plane.

3. Attach the end pieces. Where an end splash is required, the piece is usually a simple rectangle with the laminate applied to one side, one long edge, and both short edges. Fit it so that the top edge is flush with the top of the back splash and the front edge is flush with the front of the countertop. Attach it to the end of the countertop with screws and water-resistant glue. Predrill pilot holes for the screws.

If the counter has no end splash, cover the exposed edge with a special end cap. To support this piece, glue or screw ½-inch by ½-inch wood strips to the bottom and back of the countertop, flush with the end. Sand them smooth and glue the end cap in place with contact cement, following the instructions on the container.

4. Seal the bottom of the countertop with primer or wood sealer to prevent possible damage from moisture.

5. Set the countertop in place, snug against the back wall and the sidewalls. If there are gaps due to irregularities in the wall, scribe the top of the back splash with a pencil. Hold the pencil vertical and flat against the wall and run the point along the top of the back splash. Then pull the countertop out from the wall and trim away any excess on the backside of the line with a file, a block plane, or a belt sander.

6. Lay out the cutting line for the basin hole. Many manufacturers provide a template that you can trace. If you have no template, turn the basin upside down in position and trace around it. Remove the basin and draw the cutting line about ½ inch inside the tracing. This ½-inch allowance will support the rim of the basin and still clear the bowl. Leave about 2 inches of counter in front of and behind the rim of the basin.

7. Next cut a piece of 1 by 2 or similar scrap lumber 2 inches longer than the cutout for the basin hole. Attach it to the countertop by driving a single screw through the center of the board and into the center of the cutout. This board will keep the cutout from dropping through the hole before you finish sawing, which might cause the laminate to chip or break. Now drill a ¾-inch hole inside the line. Insert the blade of a saber saw into this hole and start the cut. When you reach the back splash, you may not have enough room to maneuver the saw. In that case, cut from the bottom of the countertop or use a keyhole saw. Round the corners on the cutout; square corners tend to start cracks.

8. If you are adding your own back splash to the countertop, attach it next. Drill pilot holes along the back edge of the countertop and lay down a thick bead of silicone sealant. Then set the back splash in place and drive screws up through the pilot holes to secure it. Clean up the excess sealant immediately.

9. Fasten the countertop to the vanity from below, using screws that are long enough to penetrate ½ inch into the countertop. Use self-driving screws or drill pilot holes through the cleats of the cabinets before you set the top down on them. Last of all, apply a thin bead of caulk between the countertop and the wall.

## Solid Surface Materials

Be they cast polymers or products known by the brand names Corian, Fountainhead, Avonite, and 2000X, solid surface material comes in slabs

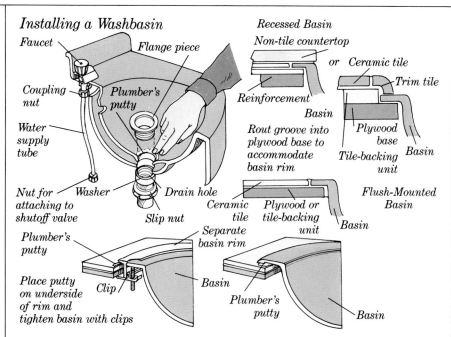

*Installing a Washbasin*

Faucet — Flange piece

Coupling nut

Plumber's putty

Water supply tube

Nut for attaching to shutoff valve — Washer — Drain hole

Slip nut

Plumber's putty

Place putty on underside of rim and tighten basin with clips — Clip — Basin

Recessed Basin
Non-tile countertop

or Ceramic tile

Trim tile

Reinforcement

Basin

Rout groove into plywood base to accommodate basin rim

Plywood base

Tile-backing unit — Basin

Ceramic tile — Plywood or tile-backing unit

Separate basin rim

Flush-Mounted Basin

Basin

Plumber's putty — Basin

that can be installed fairly easily using basic woodworking techniques.

1. If you are mounting the washbasin under the countertop, begin by installing a ¾-inch plywood base over the vanity. Cut out the basin hole. Then rout a groove around the edge of the hole so that the rim of the basin rests flush with the top of the plywood. Install the basin. You can provide extra support for it by attaching cleats under the edge of the hole.

2. Measure and cut the countertop and the back splash. Use a circular power saw with a carbide-tipped blade and cut from the backside. Wear goggles. Clamp a straightedge to the countertop to guide the saw. Protect the surface with tape.

3. To create a thicker edge, turn the top over and attach trim pieces along the edge of the bottom with an adhesive recommended by the manufacturer. Clamp the joints, let them dry overnight, and then sand them. You can attach the back splash in the same way, or you can attach it after the top is in place.

4. If you wish, you can shape the edges with a router. Carbide bits are available with which you can create soft rounds, ogees, coves, bevels, and

more elaborate shapes. Smooth the cut surfaces with abrasive paper.

5. Mark the basin hole and cut it out. Cut straight lines with a circular saw and corners with a router or a reciprocating saw, depending on the manufacturer's recommendations. Set the top in place and check for fit.

6. Attach the countertop to the plywood base or to the top of the cabinet with a sealing caulk or mastic recommended by the manufacturer. Press the top firmly into the sealant for about 10 minutes.

7. Attach the back splash if you did not do so in Step 3. Seal all the joints with a caulk recommended by the manufacturer, such as neoprene or silicone. Wipe away the excess and smooth the sealant with a damp rag wrapped around your finger.

## Stone

Marble and other natural stone must be cut and installed with specialized tools, a job that is best left to professionals. Decide how you want the washbasin mounted before you purchase the materials, because this will make a difference in the size of the basin hole, which is often cut out by the supplier. Be sure to seal the marble and maintain it to prevent stains.

## Washbasins

Wall-mounted, pedestal, and countertop washbasins are all installed in much the same way, but they are installed at different points in the sequence of construction. Basins that are recessed below a countertop must be installed before the finish material is applied. This material will either cover the rim or butt up to it for a flush surface. Basins that are mounted on a countertop are installed after the finish material. Some of these basins have a self-rim, whereas others have a separate metal rim that creates a low profile. A pedestal basin is installed after the walls are finished and the floor coverings are in place, but make sure before you cover the walls that there are studs or blocking to support the sink.

If you are replacing an old basin with a new one, you may find that the new basin does not align exactly with the old plumbing. However, you can usually accommodate the new fixture by hooking it up with flexible connectors. It is hard to crawl around under a basin, especially when it is installed in a vanity. Make your task easier by attaching as many fittings as possible to the basin before you set it into place.

### Attaching Fittings
To attach the drain fitting to the basin, first unscrew the flange piece from the top end of the drainpipe. Then screw the tightening nut down to the bottom of the threads and slip the washer and gasket over the threads all the way down to the tightening nut. Apply a ring of plumber's putty around the top edge of the drain hole. Insert the drain fitting up

*Painting the pipes white to match the pedestal sink helps to camouflage them in this family bathroom. Showrooms rarely display installed fixtures. If the look of exposed pipes bothers you, consider a vanity model washbasin rather than a pedestal sink.*

through the hole from below. Screw the flange down onto it from above. Then tighten the nut under the sink to draw the flange piece snugly down onto the putty.

Attach the faucet according to the manufacturer's instructions. A one-piece center-set faucet is the easiest to install. It has two bolts or threaded stubs; insert these down through the basin holes and attach nuts to them from below. Then connect the water supply lines to the threaded stubs. In single-control units, there are two copper supply lines attached to the faucet; connect these to the shutoff valves. Wide-set faucets are more complicated. They have a spout and two handle units, all three of which are inserted through holes in the basin or holes drilled into the countertop. Working from underneath, connect each handle unit to the spout

with flexible hosing or copper tubing provided by the manufacturer. You may have to cut the copper tubing to length. Then attach the hot and cold supply lines to their respective handle units.

Install the linkage for the pop-up drain assembly. It may be easier to do this after the basin is in place.

### Countertop Basins
A recessed basin is installed in the plywood countertop before the finish material is applied. Determine whether you want the rim of the basin to be set flush with the finish material (which is usually tile), set under it, or trimmed with quarter round ceramic trim tiles (see page 98). If the basin is to be set flush, mount it on the surface of the plywood. The rim of the basin will usually be of the same thickness as the tile. If the rim is to be recessed,

rout a groove around the edge of the basin hole, apply a bead of caulk or putty, and set the sink into the groove so that the rim sits flush with the surface of the plywood. You can also suspend a recessed basin under the plywood top with mounting clips. stalled after the finish material is applied. If the unit has an integral rim, apply a bead of caulk or plumber's putty around the edge of the countertop hole and set the basin into it. If the unit has a separate metal rim, slip the rim onto the basin first; then follow the same procedure. Secure it carefully. Then, working from underneath, slip mounting clips into the rim and tighten them with a screwdriver to hold the basin in place.

Connect the water supply lines to the shutoff valves. Then hook up the drain. If the tailpiece does not fit into the P-trap, cut it shorter or add an extension piece. Before you turn the water back on, remove the aerator attachment from the end of the faucet spout and leave if off for a few days. This will clear out any debris left in the pipes when the plumbing was roughed in.

### Wall-Mounted Basins

The basin hangs on a bracket that is provided with it. Install the bracket according to the manufacturer's instructions. Be sure to anchor it into the wall studs or into blocking installed between the studs. Use ¼-inch by 2½-inch lag screws or other heavy screws. Then lower the basin down onto the bracket, making sure that it catches securely. Straighten it with a level. Connect the drain and the water supply lines.

### Pedestal Basins

The basin and the pedestal are two separate pieces. In some installations the basin is hung on the wall first and the pedestal is installed under it. In others the pedestal is installed first

and the basin is set on top of it. If the basin is secured to the wall, make sure that there is blocking between the studs. Instead of a bracket, many models are supported on heavy lag screws inserted through holes in the back of the basin. The pedestal is bolted to the floor. If you have to drill through tile to secure the bolts, use a special tile bit or a carbide-tipped masonry bit.

The plumbing connections are the same as for other basins, except that you will usually have more space to work in, and the fittings should be attractive. If the water supply lines show, use the smooth type rather than the flexible type to give a better appearance. Use a tubing bender to shape them into a graceful arc or an S curve, being careful to avoid kinks. You can cut them to the correct length with a tubing cutter.

### Toilets

The toilet is usually installed at the very end of the project, after the walls have been painted and the flooring (except carpet) has been installed. Putting in a toilet is quite simple, no more complicated than taking one out. The technique varies with the model, so follow the manufacturer's instructions. Be sure that the rough-in dimensions for the drain and the shutoff valve are correct for the new toilet. Before you start, remove the temporary cover from the floor flange. The flange should be screwed securely to the floor.

1. Turn the new toilet bowl (or the whole toilet if it is a one-piece model) upside down and rest it on a bed of old towels or padding to protect it. Place a new wax ring around the horn of the outlet opening, pressing it firmly into place. If the closet flange is recessed below the level of the finish floor, use a wax ring with a plastic extension sleeve. The sleeve should face up when the bowl is in the upside-down position. Apply a bead of plumber's putty or bathtub caulk around the bottom edge of the bowl.

2. Slip closet bolts into the slots on each side of the floor flange. If necessary, press plumber's putty around the heads of the bolts to hold them.
3. Turn the toilet bowl right side up and set it in place on the flange, making sure that the two closet bolts slide up through the holes in the base of the toilet. Twist the bowl back and forth and rock it slightly as you press it down.
4. Make sure that the bowl is level in both directions. If necessary, slip shims of water-resistant material, such as scraps of vinyl flooring, under the base to level it. Place the washers and nuts on the closet bolts and tighten the nuts snugly. Don't overtighten them or you will crack the base. Cover the nuts with the ceramic or plastic caps provided with the toilet. You may have to trim the closet bolts with a hacksaw first, so that the caps will fit over them.
5. Install the tank according to the manufacturer's directions. Most tanks come with rubber washers and gaskets that must be put on in the proper sequence to prevent leaks. The tank will be connected to the bowl with two or three bolts. Tighten them carefully so as not to crack either piece.
6. Hook up a 12-inch water supply line between the shutoff valve and the inlet stub of the flush valve. Open the shutoff valve and let the tank fill up. Stop any leaks around the fittings by tightening the nuts at the places where they occur. Flush the toilet and watch for leaks around the base. If possible, have someone watch from under the floor, where a leak may otherwise go undetected for a long time. If there is a leak under the toilet, it means that the wax ring has slipped out of place. The only solution is to pull up the toilet and start all over again, using a new wax ring.
7. Install the toilet seat by fitting the seat bolts into the holes at the back of the bowl and securing them with washers and nuts.

# FINISHING WALLS AND FLOORS

Applying the finish materials to the walls and floor may be the most satisfying part of the whole construction project. At this point the new bathroom finally looks complete; in fact, in most cases you will have already begun to use it. Or perhaps a new finish on the walls and floor was all the old bathroom needed. New paint, tile, or other wallcovering; new flooring; and new accessories can transform a space.

Whether or not it is a part of a larger remodeling project, take care that the finishing is done accurately. Use the correct materials and tools and take the time to do a good job. You'll be looking at these surfaces every day for years.

## Walls

The most important consideration in finishing bathroom walls is to purchase materials that are suitable for use in a wet area. Check the labels carefully. Don't be shy about asking dealers for their recommendations.

Wallboard, the basic surface material for most walls and ceilings, can be finished or covered in a variety of ways. After the joints are taped and covered with wallboard compound, the surface is either sanded smooth or a layer of texture is applied. Smooth walls are desirable for easy maintenance or as a base for wallcoverings or tile. Textured surfaces create interest and can simulate various looks such as plastered adobe for a southwestern theme.

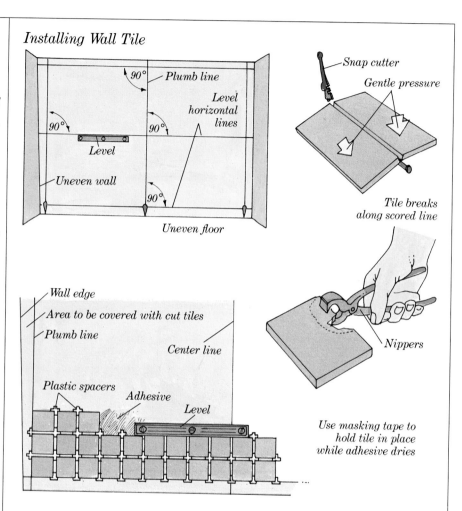

Installing Wall Tile

90° — Plumb line
Level horizontal lines
90°
90°
Level
Uneven wall
90°
Uneven floor

Snap cutter
Gentle pressure
Tile breaks along scored line

Nippers

Use masking tape to hold tile in place while adhesive dries

Wall edge
Area to be covered with cut tiles
Plumb line
Center line
Plastic spacers
Adhesive
Level

If you want smooth walls, apply at least three layers of wallboard compound over the taped joints and nail depressions; sand lightly after each coat. To be absolutely sure of a flawless surface, shine a light along the wall at a very oblique angle to accentuate any shadows caused by depressions or bumps. Inspect skylight wells carefully; bright sunlight will reveal any variations of the smooth wall.

For a textured finish, experiment on scraps of wallboard to find an effect you like. Try placing texturing compound on a large trowel and skip over the wall with it so lumps of texture form a random pattern. Mixing silica sand into the compound first and thinning it slightly will help create a more uniform look. You can vary this technique by splashing lumps of compound onto the wall,

then lightly running a large wallboard blade over them to knock the lumps down to a uniform height. For more rustic textures use a large glove or mitt to spread compound onto the wall by hand. You can also apply texture with a long-napped paint roller. Thin the texture first to a batterlike consistency.

## Paint

The walls and ceilings of most bathrooms are subject to constant moisture and humidity, so choose and apply paint carefully. Use a PVA (polyvinyl acetate) primer to seal new wallboard before applying the final coats of paint. Do not use an oil-based primer—it will raise the grain of the wallboard paper. The finish coat can be either a semigloss latex or an oil-based paint with a satin or semigloss finish. Avoid using flat paints because they do not wash easily and are more subject to wear. The finish texture of the paint can be varied by using different brushes and rollers. Roller sleeves with a very short nap, or foam rollers, produce the smoothest finish. Rollers with longer naps produce orange peel finishes. Special thickening agents can be added to the paint to create a stipple finish.

Seal new woodwork with an oil-based primer. If you paint with a roller, use a foam roller sleeve for a smooth finish with no fuzz. Use an oil-based finish coat or a high-quality latex semigloss enamel.

Previously painted surfaces must be clean, dry, and free of peeling paint. Wash them with TSP (trisodium phosphate), mixed according to package directions. If the surfaces are glossy, roughen them with sandpaper before washing them with TSP, so the new paint will adhere better. Consult a knowledgeable paint dealer for other recommendations, and always follow directions on the paint can carefully. Some paints cannot be thinned; some can be applied only in a limited range of room temperatures; and some require a certain type of brush for application. Avoid cheap paints. They have little pigment and will not stand up to normal bathroom wear. For small bathrooms subject to excessive moisture, ask the paint dealer to mix a mildewcide into the paint to prevent mildew.

To estimate the amount of paint you will need, measure the area of all the wall and ceiling surfaces you need to cover. Multiply the width by the height of each wall, and subtract the area of windows, doors, etc., from the total. Your paint dealer or the printed instructions on the paint can will tell you how much area each gallon of paint will cover.

## Wallcoverings
Choose bathroom wallcoverings with the same care used to choose paint. Avoid traditional paper wallcoverings, hand-painted papers, and natural fibers and fabrics (such as silk, grass cloth, or hemp). The most suitable wallcoverings for bathrooms are vinyls, which come in a wide array of colors, patterns, and textures. Many of them simulate authentic wallpapers and fabrics. Some are all vinyl, which are very durable and easy to maintain, but may be limited in patterns. Vinyl-coated papers are very common and have almost unlimited patterns, but the backing can tear easily. Vinyls with a fabric backing of polyester or cheesecloth are more durable. Expanded vinyls resemble fabrics or other natural textures. They are useful for covering rough walls.

Think about using wallcoverings imaginatively. For instance, wallcovering applied to the bottom half of walls, then topped with a border strip, creates an attractive wainscoting.

To estimate the amount of wallcovering you will need, measure the area of the wall and ceiling surfaces to be covered and add about 10 percent for waste and trimming. Most American products cover about 35 square feet per roll; European, or metric, wallcoverings cover about 28 square feet per roll. (A *roll* is a standard unit of measurement and may actually consist of two or three rolls packaged together.) Because dye lots or printing runs may vary, be sure to buy enough wallcovering for the entire job at one time. Check the rolls before installing to be sure the colors and patterns match.

Ask the dealer for specific recommendations about preparing the walls for installation. In most cases, the best method is to seal new wallboard with a PVA primer, then paint it with an oil-based topcoat, and apply sizing, available where wallcoverings are sold. You can apply wallcoverings directly to unpainted wallboard, but it will be impossible to remove the wallcovering at a later date without destroying the wallboard itself.

## Wood
Bathroom walls covered with natural wood are dramatic and create a warm, inviting feeling, but they must be finished carefully. Otherwise, the wood can expand and contract as moisture levels in the bathroom change. The wood can also rot over time or trap moisture behind it that can rot structural members. Improperly finished wood also attracts mold and mildew.

To prevent these problems, seal and paint the bathroom wall before covering it. Then, using a water-resistant sealer, coat the back and any hidden grooves of each piece of wood before installing it. Choose a durable type of wood—redwood, cedar, or cypress, for example—to minimize possible future problems. Apply waterproof adhesive or corrosion-resistant fasteners, such as aluminum or stainless steel nails, to the wood. Finish the exposed surface with a basic sealer and two or three coats of finish. Urethane finishes used for floors and other synthetic finishes work very well.

## Ceramic Wall Tile
Ceramic and dimensioned-stone tiles are installed in the same way. Purchase tiles designated for use on walls. These are generally thinner than floor tiles.

A successful installation depends on a smooth and stable backing—one that won't flex or deteriorate. If the walls are not exposed to direct moisture, you can attach the tiles directly to the wallboard using a mastic recommended by the tile dealer, as long as the wallboard is sound, dry, and firm. Where there is constant exposure to water—in a shower stall or a tub surround, for example—the tile should be laid over a mortar bed, which should be installed by an experienced professional, or over special tile-backing units, which you can install yourself. Some of these units are made of cement with an outer mesh of fiberglass. Others are made of lightweight composite materials. They come in panels that are installed in much the same way as wallboard: Cut them with a utility knife and nail them to the wall studs with galvanized roofing nails, or follow the manufacturer's instructions. Seal the joints with fiberglass mesh tape and water-resistant joint compound or tile adhesive.

Plan the layout carefully before you set any tiles. You need to know, before you set any tiles, whether the floor is level and straight, whether the corners are plumb, and whether there are any prominent horizontal lines with which the layout must harmonize. You also need to know how much space will be left over at the end of each row. You can cut tiles to fit the leftover space, but you have to decide where you want the cut tiles to go in order to create the most pleasing layout. If the space is narrow, it is usually better to add the amount of its width to a full tile, divide the sum in half, and use this measurement to cut both the starting tile and the end tile so that they will be equal.

There are several ways to plan the layout. One method is to first determine what prominent horizontal you want to align the grout lines with. It may be the floor, the top of the tub, a counter, or some other feature. Snap a level line across the wall at that point, using a chalk line. Measure the distance from this line, first to the bottom of the wall, and then to the highest point the tile will reach. Divide each measurement by the exact height of one tile, including grout. This will tell you the number of full tiles you will need and the size of the remaining space that must be filled with cut tiles. Then you can decide where the cut tiles should go. Do the same thing to plan the vertical layout.

Another method is to plot a tile pattern on the wall. Some tile setters use a pair of compass dividers and a pair of layout rods to do this. The rods are strips of 1 by 2, one cut to the width and the other to the height of the wall. The procedure is as follows.
1. Measure the width of the wall. At the center drop a plumb bob attached to a chalk line from the ceiling to the floor and snap a plumb line on the wall. Snap two more plumb lines close to the edges of the wall. They

will indicate whether the corners are plumb and where the narrowest measurement is. Now measure the height of the wall. Snap a level line across the wall at the center and snap two more level lines as close to the floor and the ceiling respectively as possible. They will indicate where the floor and the ceiling are not level or are not even. Check with a square to make sure that all of the angles created by the layout lines measure exactly 90 degrees.
2. Set the points of the compass divider to the width of one tile, plus one grout joint ($1/16$ to $3/16$ inch). Then walk the divider along the layout rod that represents the width of the wall, marking as you go. The space left over at the end will indicate how wide the cut tile has to be.
3. If you want to balance the layout so that there will be cut tiles of equal size at both ends, measure the last space, add the width of a full tile, and divide the result in half. Turn over the layout rod and mark that distance on each end. Then reset the dividers to the full width of a tile and a grout joint and walk them along the rod again. The spacings should come out even with the last mark. Mark the spacings on the wall by holding the rod just below the lowest horizontal line and transferring the marks; then repeat at the middle and top lines. The marks should align with the center plumb line, but not necessarily with the two outside plumb lines.
4. Repeat the process for the vertical layout, unless you are not installing tiles all the way to the ceiling. In that case you can skip the vertical layout because you can finish with a full row of tiles wherever you want.
5. If you are using special border tiles or trim pieces that are a different width from the field tiles, adjust the vertical layout rod accordingly. Mark the border tiles at each end of the rod and work out the spacings for the field tiles between these marks.
6. When the layout is complete, snap a chalk line for the first row of full tiles. Using the notched trowel

recommended by the manufacturer, spread adhesive over a small area. Try not to obliterate any guidelines. Set the tiles into the adhesive one by one, pressing them down with a slight twisting motion. Keep the adhesive from piling up in the grout joints and remove any excess immediately from the face of the tiles. Use plastic tile spacers to maintain a uniform distance between the tiles so that the grout lines will be straight. Proceed up the wall, one row at a time, until you have installed all the field tiles.
7. Fit tiles around obstacles, such as faucets, by cutting out notches with a pair of nippers.
8. When you have set all of the field tiles, set the border, trim, and cut tiles. To measure for a cut, place a full tile upside down over the gap to be filled. Mark it, leaving space for the grout lines at the top and bottom. Cut along the mark and install the tile with the cut side facing out.
9. Allow the adhesive to set overnight. You may want to use tape to hold the tiles in place while it is setting. Do all the grouting—walls, floors, and countertops—at once. See page 106, step 7 for instructions.

## Floors

Make sure that the subfloor is clean and completely free of dust and debris before you install any new flooring. Also be careful about walking on the new floor while you are installing it. Most of the damage that is done to new flooring occurs during and just after installation, before the materials have settled.

### Ceramic Floor Tile
Ceramic and dimensioned-stone tiles are installed in the same way. Ceramic floor tiles are generally thicker than wall tiles. If you have to make many large or straight cuts, you may want to rent a commercial tile saw, and you will need one in order to cut dimensioned-stone tiles. Nippers will suffice for small trim jobs. Always wear safety goggles when you use a tile saw.

There are two ways to plan a layout for floor tile. The first way is to start in the middle of the room and work outward. This method is described under Vinyl Floor Tile (see page 107). The second method is to align the tiles with the doorway and with the most prominent wall at right angles to the doorway. This method is described immediately below. You can try both methods and decide which one you like better. Make sure that the surface of the floor is clean, dry, and stable. Sand any rough surfaces and if necessary install an underlayment of particleboard or of plywood at least ½ inch thick.

1. Mark the center of the doorway and snap a chalk line from this point to the back of the room. Make sure that the line is exactly perpendicular to the threshold. Now lay a row of tiles down the length of the room, following the chalk line. Remember to allow for the width of the grout. Lay as many full tiles as you can and mark the floor at the spot where the last full tile ends. Nail a strip of wood across the end of the room so that its inside edge is aligned with this mark. Make sure that the strip of wood is exactly perpendicular to the original chalk line. The strip must be straight even if the back wall is not.

2. Lay out a horizontal row of tiles, perpendicular to the first row. Wherever the last full tile ends, nail down another strip of wood perpendicular to the first strip. Check to make sure that they form an angle of exactly 90 degrees.

3. Begin laying tiles at the intersection of the two strips. Adhesive is applied to the floor in two steps—first with the smooth edge of the trowel to help waterproof the underlayment. Then comb the adhesive with the notched edge held at about a 45-degree angle, covering a small section at a time.

4. Press each tile into place with a twisting motion. Use plastic tile spacers to keep the grout lines straight and remove excess mastic from the tiles immediately. When you have finished laying the first row, go back

*Installing Floor Tile*

*Notched trowel*    *2. Apply adhesive*    *3. Install full tiles*

*Wood strips*

*Chalk line*

*4. Mark and cut tiles*

*5. Install cut tiles*

*1. Perform layout*    *Doorway*    *6. Grout*    *Beater board*    *Rubber float*

*Grout*

to the beginning and start the next row. Continue until you have laid all of the full tiles.

5. Remove the two strips. Cut tiles to fit around obstacles and along the edges. Mark a tile for cutting by setting it upside down over the gap that it is intended to fill. Mark the back, allowing for the grout line. Then turn the tile back over and transfer the mark to the front. Cut it with a tile saw or a nipper. To install cut tiles, apply a thin layer of mastic to the floor with a smooth trowel and to the back of the tile with a notched trowel. Then press the tile into place.

6. For a firm and even installation, press down the entire surface with a floor roller or gently pound down all the tiles with a padded 2 by 4 and a mallet. Use scraps of plywood as knee boards to distribute your weight evenly. This work should be done shortly after you have completed the installation.

7. Allow the adhesive to set for 24 hours. Then apply the grout, using a rubber float. Spread it with diagonal strokes to keep the edge of the float from getting caught between the tiles. Tamp grout into all the crevices, using the handle of a toothbrush or a similar smooth tool. Wipe excess

grout from the surface of the tile with a sponge, rinsing it frequently in a bucket of clean water. Then buff the tiles with a dry cloth. One or two weeks after the grout has cured, apply a tile sealer over all the grouted joints to keep them clean and to prevent mildew from forming.

## Resilient Sheet Flooring

The underlayment for resilient flooring must be smooth, clean, and dry, with no cracks or bulges. This material is trickier than tile to install because you must take painstaking care in cutting the piece to size, and because a full roll is heavy and unwieldy. Try to select a roll that is wide enough to eliminate seams. A 6-foot width is adequate for most bathrooms, but 12-foot and even 9-foot widths may also be available.

1. Sheet flooring needs to relax before it is installed. Unroll it in another room and leave it spread out on the floor for at least 24 hours. The room where you leave it should be heated to 70 degrees.

2. The easiest way to cut a sheet to size is to make a paper template to lay over it. Tape together pieces of felt building paper until they entirely

## Installing Resilient Flooring Materials

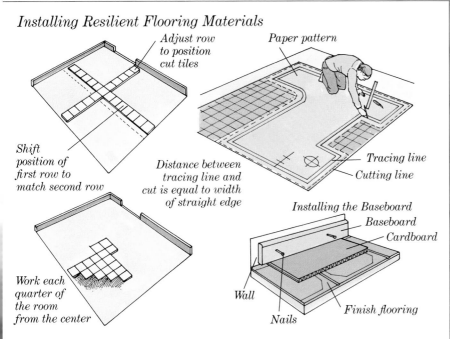

Adjust row to position cut tiles

Paper pattern

Shift position of first row to match second row

Distance between tracing line and cut is equal to width of straight edge

Tracing line

Cutting line

Work each quarter of the room from the center

Installing the Baseboard

Baseboard

Cardboard

Wall

Nails

Finish flooring

cover the floor. Leave an exposed margin of approximately ½ inch around the edge.

3. Hold a yardstick against the wall and scribe a line along the inside edge onto the paper. Repeat the operation until you have gone all the way around the room.

4. Carefully roll up the paper, take it into the other room, unroll it onto the new flooring, and tape it down. Make sure to align the design in the flooring with the edges of the pattern.

5. Hold the same yardstick that you used before along the outside edge of the tracing line on the paper pattern. Scribe a line onto the new flooring along the outside edge of the yardstick. Repeat the process until you have gone around the entire pattern. Now you have a cutting line.

6. Cut out the flooring with a utility knife. Use a straightedge to guide it. Protect the floor underneath by working on a scrap of plywood or heavy cardboard.

7. Move the new flooring into the bathroom and lay it out. Fold over half of the sheet to expose part of the floor. Spread mastic on the exposed section of floor and fold the sheet back onto it. Roll it with a floor roller.

Then fold back the other half of the sheet and repeat the process.

8. If you install baseboard molding, put a piece of cardboard or other thin material under it as you nail it in place. This leaves room for the resilient flooring to expand. Cover the exposed edge at the doorway with a metal trim piece.

## Vinyl Floor Tile

Vinyl floor tiles are easy to install, but they must be laid very carefully on a bathroom floor because poorly laid tiles will admit water into the joints. The underlayment must be smooth, clean, and free of bulges. It is advisable to seal it with wood sealer or primer. Plan the layout carefully, taking into account the same considerations as you would in planning a layout for ceramic tile. The following method will help you to design a symmetrical layout. Compare it with the layout described on page 106 and choose the one you prefer.

1. Find the center of each of the four bathroom walls. Snap a chalk line on the floor between the center points of the north and south walls. Repeat the process with the east and west walls. The chalk lines should intersect at an

angle of exactly 90 degrees. If they do not, adjust them accordingly.

2. Use the following method to achieve even rows of tile with identical borders. Lay one full row of tiles along either line, from wall to wall, without applying any mastic. If a space that is smaller than half a tile remains at the end of a row, remove the last full tile. Measure the new space, divide the measurement in half, and insert a gap of that size at the beginning and end of the row. Adjust the row accordingly. If the original space was wider than half a tile, leave it. A single end row of that width will not be very noticeable.

3. Now set out a second row of tiles perpendicular to the first. Align this second row of tiles with the edges of the center tile in the first row, and set it as close to the second chalk line as possible. Use the procedure described in step 2 to determine how you will handle the leftover space. Then move the entire first row until it is perfectly aligned with the second row. Snap new chalk lines to reflect the revised layout.

4. Using the mastic recommended by the tile manufacturer, set the four center tiles in place. Then start with the quartile that is farthest from the door and fill it in with tiles. Apply mastic to a small area at a time, to keep it from drying out and losing adhesion. Use only full tiles and work toward the walls in the sequence shown above. Cut tiles to fit around obstacles. If the mastic oozes up between the tiles, wipe it off immediately with a damp rag.

5. When you have finished laying all the full tiles in the quartile, cut the tiles for the border. Lay each tile upside down over the gap that it will fill and mark it on the back. Measure and cut each border tile individually in case the wall is not straight. When you have cut all the border tiles, set them in place. Complete the other three quartiles in the same way.

6. Apply silicone sealant around the bases of all of the fixtures. You should be able to walk on the new floor within 24 hours.

# INSTALLING FINISHING TOUCHES

*Accessories and finish details must be chosen carefully so they enhance, rather than detract, from the overall effect. They are often prominent features of the design and must, therefore, be installed straight and true. Accessories are also subject to heavy daily use, and in some cases are the first line of defense against moisture damage.*

Installing the finishing touches can be the most enjoyable and exhilarating part of remodeling. The end of the project is in sight; most of the tasks are simple and finishing each one brings a sense of finality. You might try shopping for accessories in interesting shops with dazzling showrooms, or in department stores, or home centers that you probably would enjoy seeing anyway.

## Window Treatments

Blinds in a bathroom should be high quality, with cords that resist moisture damage and metal parts that won't corrode. Most blinds, whether mini-, micro-, or regular sized, are installed by attaching brackets to the wall and hanging the blind on them. Each bracket is held to the wall with two screws. To determine bracket locations, hold the blind in various places and see how the top, bottom, and sides line up with the window. When the blind is in position, mark where the two ends line up on the window sash, trim, or wall. Then set down the blind, hold each support bracket so it will be positioned at the end of the blind rail, and mark where the screw

holes line up on the window sash, trim, or wall. Use a hammer and nail to make a small pilot hole for each screw. Then screw the brackets to the wall. If a screw will not penetrate solid wood—for instance, where there is no framing behind the wallboard—remove the screw, enlarge the screw hole to ¼-inch diameter with a drill, and insert a plastic wall anchor or expansion bolt in the hole. Then put the bracket back in place and drive the screw through it into the anchor or bolt.

Curtain rods, like blinds, are held in place by brackets that are attached to the wall with screws. To install brackets, hold the curtain rod in place and mark where brackets must be positioned to hold it. Attach brackets to the wall by following the above instructions for blinds.

Stained glass windows add beauty to a bathroom, provide visual privacy, and enhance security. Some stained glass panels are installed right into the window sash in place of the regular glass pane. The sash is set into place at the time the window is installed. Other stained glass windows are hung as panels in front of a standard window. One way to install such a panel is to suspend it in front of the window from chains attached to hooks in the wall or ceiling. The chains should be corrosion resistant and the hooks should be screwed into wall studs or ceiling joists. Using a chain at each side of the panel, rather than one chain, adds strength and keeps the panel from tilting or swaying.

## Towel Bars

Installation techniques for towel bars vary with the type of design. Some towel bars have concealed brackets that are attached to the wall first; the bar is then slipped onto them and secured with a hidden set screw. Others have wood or metal flanges at the ends of the bar that are held to

the wall with face screws that are either exposed or concealed with small plugs. The best installations secure screws to wood framing behind the wall. Installing wood blocking between the studs, before the walls are closed in, is the most secure way to provide backing for the towel bars. Otherwise, use expansion bolts or plastic wall anchors to secure the screws where the brackets are installed between studs.

## Grab Bars

Grab bars, unlike towel bars, are designed specifically to support the full weight of a person. They consist of metal tubing, usually with a brushed stainless steel finish or with painted finishes in a variety of designer colors. Fasteners are concealed and all corners and terminations are rounded for safety. Configurations may vary from a straight bar to complex shapes that wrap around corners or provide continuous support around a bathroom fixture. Many lengths and shapes are available as stock items, but you can also custom-make a shape from prefabricated parts or have a special shape made to order.

Grab bars attach to the wall with support flanges. Each flange is secured to the wall with three screws, usually 2 to 3 inches long. The flange and screws are concealed with a cover plate that slips back over the flange. The screws must penetrate the wood framing behind the wallcovering, so it is important to install blocking between studs before covering up the walls. Drill a pilot hole for each screw, smaller than the diameter of the screw. To drill through tile, use a tile bit or a bit with a carbide tip. It should be slightly larger than the diameter of the screw shank. Use a squirt bottle to train a steady stream of water on the bit as you drill to prevent overheating and to flush away tile particles. After drilling through the tile and backing, use the smaller diameter wood bit to complete the drilling into the wood framing. If you are installing a grab bar in a shower or other wet area, apply a small bead of silicone caulking around each pilot hole before attaching the support flange. After screwing the flanges securely to the wall, slip the cover plate over each one and secure it in position with the set screw provided. Follow any other instructions provided by the manufacturer.

## Shower Doors

You can install shower doors for most standard tub installations or simple shower stalls yourself, but doors that are integrated into full glass wall units should be installed by professionals. Most tub enclosures consist of two side rails that are attached to the walls, a top rail that rests on them and holds up the doors, and a bottom rail that provides a water barrier along the top of the bathtub rim. The bottom rail is usually installed first. Begin by measuring the exact distance from wall to wall along the top of the bathtub rim. Then cut the bottom rail to this length, using a hack saw and miter box or a power miter saw with a carbide-tipped blade. Install the vinyl gasket or bead on the bottom of the rail and set it into place. Then hold each side rail in place, making sure it interlocks over the bottom rail and is plumb. Mark the locations for the screws on the walls and remove the rails. Using the same techniques for drilling through tile as described above for grab bars, drill holes for the screws. Then screw the side rails to the walls. Cut the top rail to length and set it down onto the side rails and hang the doors on it, as described in the manufacturer's instructions. Finally, run a bead of silicone caulk along the inside of each side rail

*An adjustable sink—the front lever raises the pedestal and the pipes are flexible—solves the problems that arise when people of different heights use the same bathroom.*

where it meets the wall. Do not apply caulking along the inside edge of the bottom rail, or water will not be able to flow under it back into the bathtub.

The door for a shower stall is installed with similar techniques. When installing the bottom rail, however, apply a bead of caulking inside the exterior edge to augment the vinyl gasket. Most models have a special sleeve on the side rail where the door is hinged so it can be adjusted to fit the exact width of the door opening.

## Accessories

Soap dishes, toilet-paper holders, and similar accessories are secured to the wall with screws. Most fixtures are also secured with screws. They are not heavy enough to require solid-wood backing behind the walls, but

where there is no wood backing the screws should be secured with plastic wall anchors or expansion bolts. Many toilet-paper holders are recessed into the wall and held in place by screws driven through the back of the housing. To accomplish this, cut a rough opening into the wallboard. Then set the holder in place to test the size of the opening. As there is no support directly behind the holder to drive the screws into, install a short 2 by 4 or similar blocking between the studs at the back of the rough opening. Secure it to the studs with screws or hold it in place with screws driven through the wallboard on the opposite side of the wall. Countersink and spackle the screw heads. Then place the holder in position and secure it with screws driven into the new blocking.

# PHOTOGRAPHY ACKNOWLEDGMENTS

## Homeowners

Special thanks to the following people who so graciously allowed us to photograph their homes.

Cy, Judith, and Ana Berlowitz
Lee and Deborah Bond-Upson
Pete and Sue Bowser
James and Pamela Cameron
Kathy and Phil Doherty
Alan H. and Riitta H. Gluskin
Michael and Taeko Jenkins
Carolyn Klebanoff
Gloria Knuckles
Gary and Sharon Lindahl
Charles B. Long
Sharyn McCoy
Nancy and Tom Mavrides
Patricia and Rudy Meiswinkle
Sarah S. and James G. Mills
Barbara and Howard Norton
Mr. and Mrs. Michael F. O'Neill
Maxim D. Schrogin and Karen Harber
Nan Schurkus
Harry Specht
Victoria Stone

## Featured Bathrooms

Special thanks to the following individuals and businesses who generously allowed us to photograph their work.

Front cover, page 6
Designers: Homeowner; Rick Sambol, Kitchen Consultants
Builder: MacDougall Construction

Pages 1, 11
Designer: Agnes Bourne

Pages 3, 24, 32, 53, 60
Designers: Rick Sambol, Kitchen Consultants; Debra Gutierrez Interiors
Builders: Cam Fraser Construction; Bob Spoor Masonry

Pages 5, 59
Designer: Homeowner
Builders: Tom Banfield; Fran Segal

Pages 9, 51
Designers: Homeowner; Carlene Anderson
Builder: Dan Smith

Page 15
Designer: Leonard D. Grotta

Pages 18, 48
Designers: Homeowner; Rick Sambol, Kitchen Consultants
Builder: MacDougall Construction

Page 23
Builder: Larry Hayden, Federal Building Company

Pages 28, 109
Designer: Westor Mattews, Fitschen Associates
Builder: Dei Russi Tile and Construction

Pages 29, 66
Designer: Rick Sambol, Kitchen Consultants
Builders: Denis Healy; Chuck Bond; Bob Spoor Masonry

Page 30
Designers: Homeowner; Terry Smith; Carlene Anderson
Builder: Randy Welker

Page 31
Designers: Homeowner; Terry Smith; Carlene Anderson
Builder: Randy Welker
Stained Glass: Sabina Frank

Page 33, 82
Designers: Sheree Douglas, D.C. Douglas Interiors; Alice Johnson; Sharyn McCoy

Pages 37, 72, back cover (top left)
Designer: Jim Miller
Builder: Jim Martin, Lignum Vitae

Page 38
Designer: Barbara McQueen, Pizazz Interior Design
Builder: Sam Davis, Sam-Cin Company

Page 39
Designer: Homeowner
Builder: Dei Rossi Tile and Construction

Page 41
Designers: Nancy Barnard, Interior Designer; George Swallow, Architect
Builder: Dennis Lindstom

Pages 42, 71
Designer: Mary Plunt Design
Builder: Superior Home Remodeling

Page 44
Designer: Sheree Douglas, D.C. Douglas Interiors

Page 47, back cover (bottom right)
Designer: Victoria Stone
Builder: Paul Chow

Page 54
Designer and Builder: Superior Home Remodeling

Pages 55, 68, back cover (top right)
Designer and Builder: Tom Banfield, Banfield Design and Construction

Pages 56, 57
Designers: Judith Berlowitz; Andrew Beckerman
Builder: William L. Eggert

Pages 65, 84
Designer: Homeowner

Page 75
Designers: Rick Sambol, Kitchen Consultants; Karen Carroll Interiors
Builders: Denis Healy; Chuck Bond; Michael Skeels

Pages 78, 79
Designers: Pamela Cameron, Uniquely Yours; Paul Kline, House of Kitchens
Builder: Wilson Way Builders
Shower Glass Design: Marilyn Hajjar, Artability

Page 81
Designer: Deborah Rae Interiors

Page 93
Designer: Homeowner

Back cover (bottom left)
Designer: Nancy Barnard, Interior Designer
Builder: Dennis Lindstrom

# INDEX

## *U.S. / Metric Measure Conversion Chart*

| | *Formulas for Exact Measures* | | | | *Rounded Measures for Quick Reference* | | |
|---|---|---|---|---|---|---|---|
| | *Symbol* | *When you know:* | *Multiply by:* | *To find:* | | | |
| *Mass (Weight)* | oz | ounces | 28.35 | grams | 1 oz | | = 30 g |
| | lb | pounds | 0.45 | kilograms | 4 oz | | = 115 g |
| | g | grams | 0.035 | ounces | 8 oz | | = 225 g |
| | kg | kilograms | 2.2 | pounds | 16 oz | = 1 lb | = 450 g |
| | | | | | 32 oz | = 2 lb | = 900 g |
| | | | | | 36 oz | = 2¼ lb | = 1000 g (1 kg) |
| *Volume* | tsp | teaspoons | 5.0 | milliliters | ¼ tsp | = 1/24 oz | = 1 ml |
| | tbsp | tablespoons | 15.0 | milliliters | ½ tsp | = 1/12 oz | = 2 ml |
| | fl oz | fluid ounces | 29.57 | milliliters | 1 tsp | = 1/6 oz | = 5 ml |
| | c | cups | 0.24 | liters | 1 tbsp | = ½ oz | = 15 ml |
| | pt | pints | 0.47 | liters | 1 c | = 8 oz | = 250 ml |
| | qt | quarts | 0.95 | liters | 2 c (1 pt) | = 16 oz | = 500 ml |
| | gal | gallons | 3.785 | liters | 4 c (1 qt) | = 32 oz | = 1 liter |
| | ml | milliliters | 0.034 | fluid ounces | 4 qt (1 gal) | = 128 oz | = 3¾ liter |
| *Length* | in. | inches | 2.54 | centimeters | ⅜ in. | = 1 cm | |
| | ft | feet | 30.48 | centimeters | 1 in. | = 2.5 cm | |
| | yd | yards | 0.9144 | meters | 2 in. | = 5 cm | |
| | mi | miles | 1.609 | kilometers | 2½ in. | = 6.5 cm | |
| | km | kilometers | 0.621 | miles | 12 in. (1 ft) | = 30 cm | |
| | m | meters | 1.094 | yards | 1 yd | = 90 cm | |
| | cm | centimeters | 0.39 | inches | 100 ft | = 30 m | |
| | | | | | 1 mi | = 1.6 km | |
| *Temperature* | °F | Fahrenheit | 5/9 (after subtracting 32) | Celsius | 32° F | = 0° C | |
| | | | | | 68°F | = 20° C | |
| | °C | Celsius | 9/5 (then add 32) | Fahrenheit | 212° F | = 100° C | |
| *Area* | in.² | square inches | 6.452 | square centimeters | 1 in.² | = 6.5 cm² | |
| | ft² | square feet | 929.0 | square centimeters | 1 ft² | = 930 cm² | |
| | yd² | square yards | 8361.0 | square centimeters | 1 yd² | = 8360 cm² | |
| | a. | acres | 0.4047 | hectares | 1 a. | = 4050 m² | |